Securing the Internet of Things (IoT): Cybersecurity of Connected Devices

Summary

1. Introduction to IoT Security

Internet of Things and its significance.

The proliferation of IoT devices in various sectors.

The security implications associated with the interconnected nature of IoT.

2. IoT Device Vulnerabilities

Common vulnerabilities in IoT devices

The security risks posed by insecure firmware, weak authentication, and lack of encryption

Examples of real-world IoT security breaches

3. Securing IoT Networks

Challenges of securing IoT networks

The role of firewalls, intrusion detection systems, and network segmentation in IoT security

Best practices for safeguarding communication between IoT devices

4. Data Privacy in IoT

Address the sensitive nature of data generated by IoT devices

Privacy concerns related to the collection and storage of IoT data

Encryption and anonymization techniques to protect user privacy

5. IoT Security Standards and Regulations

Overview of existing standards and regulations specific to IoT security

Compliance requirements and the importance of adhering to industry standards

Global efforts to establish a unified framework for IoT security

6. IoT Authentication and Access Control

The significance of robust authentication mechanisms for IoT devices

The role of access control in limiting unauthorized access to IoT systems

The challenges of managing credentials for a multitude of interconnected devices

7. IoT Firmware Security

Security considerations of IoT device firmware

The importance of secure boot processes and firmware updates

Exploring techniques for ensuring the integrity and authenticity of IoT device firmware

8. IoT Ethical Hacking

The concept of ethical hacking for IoT security

The role of penetration testing in identifying vulnerabilities in IoT devices and networks

Responsible disclosure practices in the IoT ecosystem

9. IoT Security Best Practices

Comprehensive set of best practices for securing IoT deployment

IoT Security Best Practices: device management, secure coding practices, and ongoing monitoring

IoT Security Best Practices: practical tips for both

manufacturers and end-users

10. Future Trends in IoT Security

Explore emerging technologies that could impact the future of IoT security

Potential advancements in blockchain, artificial intelligence, and edge computing

Anticipating of challenges and opportunities as IoT continues to evolve

11. Case Studies and Lessons Learned

Real-world case studies of successful IoT security implementations

Highlight lessons learned from notable IoT security incidents

Key takeaways for readers to apply in their own IoT security strategies

Bibliography

Summary

The Internet of Things (IoT) refers to the network of interconnected physical devices, vehicles, appliances, and other objects embedded with sensors, software, and network connectivity. These devices can collect and exchange data, enabling them to interact with each other and with their environment. The significance of IoT lies in its ability to enhance efficiency, provide valuable insights through data analytics, and improve automation in various sectors, ranging from healthcare and agriculture to smart cities and industrial processes.

The use of IoT devices has proliferated across diverse sectors, including healthcare, agriculture, transportation, manufacturing, and smart homes. These devices offer benefits such as real-time monitoring, predictive maintenance, and improved decision-making. However, the widespread deployment of IoT devices also raises security concerns due to the interconnected nature of these systems.

The interconnected nature of IoT introduces security challenges as it expands the attack surface. Vulnerabilities in one device can potentially compromise the entire network, leading to data breaches, unauthorized access, and disruptions to critical services.

Common vulnerabilities in IoT devices include insecure firmware, weak authentication mechanisms, insufficient encryption, and susceptibility to physical tampering. These vulnerabilities can be exploited by attackers to gain unauthorized access, manipulate data, or launch attacks on other devices.

Insecure firmware can be a major security risk, as it may contain vulnerabilities that can be exploited by attackers. Weak authentication mechanisms can lead to unauthorized access, while the lack of encryption can expose sensitive data to interception and manipulation.

Real-world examples of IoT security breaches include incidents where attackers compromised smart home devices, industrial control systems, or healthcare devices to gain unauthorized access, manipulate data, or disrupt operations. These breaches highlight the need for robust security measures in IoT deployments.

Securing IoT networks is challenging due to the diverse nature of devices, varying communication protocols, and the sheer volume of data generated. Additionally, many IoT devices have resource constraints, making it difficult to implement robust security measures.

Firewalls, intrusion detection systems (IDS), and network segmentation play crucial roles in IoT security. Firewalls help filter and monitor traffic, IDS detects unusual behavior, and network segmentation limits the impact of a breach by isolating compromised devices from the rest of the network.

Implementing strong encryption protocols, ensuring secure key management, and regularly updating device firmware are key best practices for safeguarding communication between IoT devices. Additionally, using secure communication protocols such as TLS/SSL enhances the integrity and confidentiality of data.

Data generated by IoT devices often includes sensitive information about individuals, their habits, and their environments. Protecting this data is crucial to maintain user privacy and prevent unauthorized access.

Privacy concerns arise when IoT devices collect and store personal information without adequate safeguards. Unauthorized access to this data can lead to identity theft, stalking, or other malicious activities.

Implementing end-to-end encryption and anonymizing personally identifiable information (PII) are essential techniques to protect user privacy. These measures ensure that even if data is intercepted, it remains unintelligible without proper decryption keys.

Various organizations and consortia have developed standards and regulations to address IoT security. Examples include the IoT Security Foundation's guidelines and the NIST Cybersecurity Framework. Compliance with these standards is essential for ensuring a baseline level of security.

Adhering to industry standards is crucial for establishing a common framework for IoT security. Compliance requirements help ensure that IoT devices and systems meet minimum security standards, reducing the risk of vulnerabilities and enhancing overall cybersecurity posture.

Global efforts, such as collaborations between industry stakeholders, governments, and international organizations, aim to establish a unified framework for IoT security. These efforts seek to create a cohesive set of guidelines that can be universally adopted to enhance the security of IoT ecosystems.

Robust authentication mechanisms, such as multi-factor authentication, are crucial for ensuring that only authorized users and devices can access IoT systems. Weak authentication can lead to unauthorized access and compromise the integrity of the entire IoT network.

Access control mechanisms, including role-based access control (RBAC) and least privilege principles, help limit unauthorized access to IoT systems. Properly configured access controls ensure that users and devices have only the necessary permissions for their designated roles.

Managing credentials for a large number of interconnected devices is challenging. Secure credential storage, regular updates, and the use of secure key management practices are essential to mitigate the risk of credential-based attacks.

IoT device firmware security is critical to prevent unauthorized access and exploitation. Secure boot processes, secure coding practices, and regular firmware updates are key elements in ensuring the integrity and security of IoT device firmware.

Secure boot processes ensure that only authenticated and unaltered firmware is loaded during device startup. Regular firmware updates, including security patches, help address vulnerabilities and improve the overall security of IoT devices.

Digital signatures, cryptographic checksums, and code signing are techniques used to ensure the integrity and authenticity of IoT device firmware. These measures help verify that the firmware has not been tampered with and is from a trusted source.

Ethical hacking involves authorized testing and evaluation of systems to identify vulnerabilities. In the context of IoT security, ethical hackers play a crucial role in identifying and addressing weaknesses in devices and networks.

Penetration testing involves simulating real-world attacks to identify vulnerabilities and weaknesses in IoT devices and networks. This proactive approach helps organizations identify and fix security issues before they can be exploited by malicious actors.

Highlight responsible disclosure practices in the IoT ecosystem:

Responsible disclosure involves ethical hackers reporting identified vulnerabilities to the device manufacturers or relevant stakeholders before making them public. This practice allows for timely patches and fixes without putting users at risk.

We have to provide a comprehensive set of best practices for securing IoT deployments:

- Implement strong authentication mechanisms, including multi-factor authentication.
- Regularly update and patch firmware to address known vulnerabilities.
- Encrypt communication between devices to protect data integrity and confidentiality.
- Employ access control mechanisms to limit unauthorized access.
- Monitor and log IoT device activities to detect and respond to anomalies.
- Conduct regular security audits and penetration testing.
- Educate users and administrators about security best practices.
- Establish a secure supply chain for IoT devices to prevent tampering during production.

We have to cover topics such as device management, secure coding practices, and ongoing monitoring:

- Implement robust device management protocols for secure provisioning and decommissioning.

- Enforce secure coding practices during the development of IoT device firmware and software.
- Continuously monitor and assess the security posture of IoT devices and networks.
- Use secure update mechanisms to deploy patches and updates to devices.

We have to include practical tips for both manufacturers and end-users:

- Manufacturers should prioritize security in the design phase, conduct security testing, and provide regular firmware updates.
- End-users should change default passwords, update device firmware regularly, and be cautious about sharing sensitive information.

Future Trends in IoT Security:

Exploring emerging technologies that could impact the future of IoT security:

- Blockchain for secure and tamper-proof data storage.
- Artificial intelligence for advanced threat detection and mitigation.
- Edge computing for processing data closer to the source, reducing latency and improving security.

Discussing potential advancements in blockchain, artificial intelligence, and edge computing:

- Blockchain can enhance the integrity of data by providing a decentralized and tamper-proof ledger.
- Artificial intelligence can improve anomaly detection and response capabilities.
- Edge computing can reduce the attack surface by processing data locally, minimizing the need for data to travel over the network.

We have to anticipate challenges and opportunities as IoT continues to evolve:

Challenges include addressing the security of legacy devices, managing the increasing complexity of IoT ecosystems, and establishing industry-wide standards. Opportunities lie in leveraging emerging technologies to enhance security and adopting proactive security measures in IoT design and deployment.

We have to examine cases where organizations successfully implemented robust security measures, mitigated vulnerabilities, and responded effectively to security incidents.

We have to highlight lessons learned from notable IoT security incidents by:

Identifying common themes and lessons from high-profile IoT security incidents, emphasizing the importance of proactive security measures, timely response, and continuous improvement.

The key takeaways in regards to IoT security strategies are:

- Prioritize security in the design and development of IoT systems.
- Regularly update and patch firmware to address vulnerabilities.
- Implement strong authentication and access control mechanisms.
- Monitor IoT devices for suspicious activities and anomalies.
- Foster collaboration between industry stakeholders for a unified approach to IoT security.

1. Introduction to IoT Security

Internet of Things and its significance.

The Internet of Things (IoT) has emerged as a transformative force, ushering in an era where everyday objects are imbued with intelligence and connectivity. This interconnected web of devices, ranging from smart home appliances to industrial sensors, has the potential to revolutionize how we live, work, and interact with the world around us. However, the unprecedented growth of the IoT comes with inherent challenges, particularly in the realm of security. In this comprehensive introduction, we will delve into the multifaceted landscape of the Internet of Things, defining its essence, exploring its significance, and unraveling the intricate tapestry of IoT security.

Defining the Internet of Things (IoT). Origins and Evolution.

The concept of the Internet of Things traces its roots to the early 2000s, although the vision of a connected world has deeper historical roots. The evolution of IoT can be seen as a natural progression from the integration of computing into everyday objects. Kevin Ashton, a British technologist, is often credited with coining the term "Internet of Things" in 1999, envisioning a future where physical objects would be equipped with sensors, enabling them to communicate and share data seamlessly.

Essence of IoT:

At its core, the Internet of Things refers to the interconnection of a vast network of devices that communicate with each other to collect, exchange, and act upon data. These devices, often embedded with sensors and actuators, are capable of generating and receiving information, creating an intricate web of connectivity. The essence of IoT lies in the ability of these devices to operate intelligently, making decisions based on the data they collect, and contributing to a more efficient and interconnected world.

Diversity of IoT Devices:

The spectrum of IoT devices is remarkably diverse, encompassing various sectors and industries. From consumer-oriented devices like smart thermostats and fitness trackers to industrial applications such as smart factories and agricultural sensors, the reach of IoT is expansive. Each device within the IoT ecosystem serves a specific purpose, contributing to the overall connectivity and functionality of the network.

Connectivity and Communication Protocols:

The seamless functioning of IoT relies on robust connectivity and communication protocols. Devices within the IoT ecosystem communicate through wired or wireless networks, utilizing protocols such as MQTT (Message Queuing Telemetry Transport), CoAP (Constrained Application Protocol), and HTTP (Hypertext Transfer Protocol). These protocols facilitate the transfer of data between devices, forming the backbone of the IoT infrastructure.

II. Significance of the Internet of Things

A. Transformation of Industries:

One of the key aspects of the significance of IoT lies in its transformative impact on industries. Across sectors such as healthcare, agriculture, manufacturing, and transportation,

IoT technologies have introduced efficiencies, reduced costs, and enabled data-driven decision-making. In healthcare, for example, IoT devices can monitor patient vital signs in real-time, enhancing the quality of care and allowing for timely interventions.

B. Enhanced User Experience:

In the consumer realm, IoT has redefined the way individuals interact with their surroundings. Smart homes equipped with IoT devices offer unprecedented levels of convenience and automation. From voice-activated assistants to connected appliances, IoT has woven itself into the fabric of daily life, promising a more streamlined and personalized user experience.

C. Data-Driven Insights:

The proliferation of IoT devices has led to the generation of vast amounts of data. This data, often referred to as Big Data, holds the potential for extracting valuable insights. By analyzing the data generated by IoT devices, businesses and organizations can make informed decisions, optimize processes, and gain a deeper understanding of user behavior and preferences.

D. Economic Impact:

The economic impact of IoT is substantial, contributing to the growth of industries and the creation of new business models. IoT technologies open avenues for innovation, creating opportunities for startups and established enterprises alike. As the IoT ecosystem continues to expand, it is anticipated to generate significant economic value, driving advancements in technology and fostering a culture of innovation.

E. Societal Implications:

Beyond the economic and industrial implications, the Internet of Things carries profound societal implications. The integration of IoT into smart cities, for instance, promises improved urban planning, resource management, and sustainability. Additionally, IoT applications in areas such as environmental monitoring and disaster response underscore its potential to address global challenges and contribute to the betterment of society.

III. The Complex Landscape of IoT Security

A. Unique Security Challenges:

While the Internet of Things presents a myriad of opportunities, it also introduces unique security challenges. The sheer scale and diversity of IoT devices make them susceptible to a wide range of cyber threats. Insecure devices, inadequate authentication mechanisms, and vulnerabilities in communication protocols pose significant risks to the integrity and confidentiality of IoT ecosystems.

B. Privacy Concerns:

The vast amount of data generated by IoT devices raises critical privacy concerns. Personal information, behavioral patterns, and even location data can be collected and exploited if not adequately protected. Striking a balance between the convenience offered by IoT and safeguarding user privacy remains a central challenge in the development and deployment of IoT technologies.

C. Proliferation of Vulnerable Devices:

One of the inherent challenges of IoT security is the proliferation of potentially vulnerable devices. Many IoT devices, especially those designed for cost-effectiveness, may lack robust security features. This creates a scenario where a compromised device within the ecosystem can serve as a gateway for attackers to infiltrate the entire network.

D. Interconnected Threat Landscape:

The interconnected nature of IoT devices amplifies the impact of security breaches. A compromised device can not only jeopardize its immediate functionality but may also pose a threat to other devices within the network. The ripple effect of security incidents in the IoT landscape underscores the need for comprehensive and holistic security measures.

E. Evolving Nature of Threats:

As IoT technologies advance, so do the tactics employed by malicious actors. Threats such as ransomware, distributed denial-of-service (DDoS) attacks, and unauthorized access constantly evolve to exploit vulnerabilities in IoT ecosystems. The dynamic nature of these threats requires continuous adaptation and innovation in IoT security measures.

IV. Conclusion

In this extensive exploration of the Internet of Things and its security landscape, we have defined the essence of IoT, emphasizing its transformative significance in various domains. The interconnected web of devices, from the mundane to the sophisticated, forms the backbone of the IoT ecosystem, promising a future where data-driven insights, enhanced user experiences, and societal advancements are the norm.

However, the significance of IoT is intrinsically linked to the security challenges it presents. The complexity of securing a diverse array of devices, coupled with the evolving nature of cyber threats, demands a proactive and multifaceted approach to IoT security. As we navigate this intricate landscape, it becomes imperative to address the unique challenges posed by IoT and forge a path towards a secure and resilient connected future.

In subsequent chapters, we will delve deeper into the specific dimensions of IoT security, exploring strategies, best practices, and innovative approaches to safeguarding the integrity, confidentiality, and availability of IoT ecosystems. From securing communication protocols to addressing privacy concerns, each facet of IoT security plays a pivotal role in ensuring the continued growth and positive impact of the Internet of Things.

The proliferation of IoT devices in various sectors.

The proliferation of Internet of Things (IoT) devices has become a defining characteristic of our rapidly evolving technological landscape. From smart homes to industrial settings, healthcare facilities to agricultural fields, the deployment of IoT devices spans a myriad of sectors, each bringing unique challenges and opportunities. In this extensive exploration, we will delve into the expansive reach of IoT devices, examining their impact on diverse sectors, the transformative potential they hold, and the implications for security, efficiency, and innovation.

I. Smart Homes: Redefining Everyday Living

A. Connected Living Spaces:

The integration of IoT devices in residential settings has transformed traditional homes into smart, connected living spaces. Smart thermostats, lighting systems, security cameras, and voice-activated assistants have become commonplace, offering residents unprecedented control, convenience, and energy efficiency.

B. Home Automation and Entertainment:

IoT-enabled home automation systems allow users to seamlessly control and monitor various aspects of their homes remotely. From adjusting the thermostat to managing smart appliances, the connected home ensures a personalized and streamlined living experience. Entertainment systems, too, have undergone a revolution with IoT, offering immersive and interconnected audio-visual experiences.

C. Security and Surveillance:

The adoption of IoT devices in home security has significantly enhanced safety measures. Smart doorbell cameras, motion sensors, and smart locks provide real-time monitoring and alerts, empowering residents with the ability to secure their homes remotely. However, the proliferation of such devices also raises concerns about privacy and data security.

II. Industrial IoT (IIoT): Transforming Manufacturing and Industry

A. Smart Factories and Industry 4.0:

In the industrial landscape, the integration of IoT devices has given rise to the concept of Industry 4.0. Smart factories leverage IoT technologies to optimize manufacturing processes, monitor equipment health, and enhance overall operational efficiency. Connected sensors on machines enable predictive maintenance, reducing downtime and ensuring continuous production.

B. Supply Chain and Logistics:

IoT devices play a crucial role in optimizing supply chain and logistics operations. RFID tags, GPS trackers, and sensors on shipping containers provide real-time visibility into the movement of goods, allowing for more efficient inventory management, reduced delays, and enhanced traceability.

C. Energy Management:

Industrial IoT extends to energy management, where smart meters and sensors monitor energy consumption in real-time. This data enables businesses to implement energy-efficient practices, reduce costs, and contribute to sustainability goals.

III. Healthcare: Revolutionizing Patient Care

A. Remote Patient Monitoring:

IoT devices in healthcare facilitate remote patient monitoring, enabling healthcare professionals to track vital signs, medication adherence, and overall patient well-being. This not only enhances the quality of patient care but also reduces the need for frequent hospital visits.

B. Wearable Health Tech:

Wearable devices equipped with IoT capabilities have become integral to personal health management. From fitness trackers monitoring physical activity to smartwatches measuring vital signs, these devices empower individuals to take a proactive approach to their health.

C. Medical Asset Tracking:

Hospitals utilize IoT for tracking medical assets such as equipment, medications, and even personnel. This improves operational efficiency, reduces errors, and ensures that critical resources are readily available when needed.

IV. Agriculture: Precision Farming for Sustainable Practices

A. Smart Farming Equipment:

The agriculture sector has witnessed a surge in the adoption of IoT devices for precision farming. Smart tractors, drones, and sensors collect data on soil conditions, crop health, and weather patterns, allowing farmers to make data-driven decisions for optimal yield.

B. Livestock Monitoring:

IoT-enabled devices assist in monitoring the health and well-being of livestock. Wearable sensors on animals can track vital metrics, providing early detection of illnesses and ensuring the overall health of the herd.

C. Crop Management:

IoT devices aid in precise crop management by delivering insights into irrigation needs, pest control, and crop harvesting times. This targeted approach improves resource efficiency and sustainability in agriculture.

V. Retail: Enhancing Customer Experiences

A. Inventory Management:

Retailers leverage IoT devices for efficient inventory management. RFID tags, sensors, and connected cameras enable real-time tracking of stock levels, reducing instances of stockouts and overstock.

B. Personalized Shopping Experiences:

IoT contributes to personalized shopping experiences through beacons and smart shelves. These devices provide location-based promotions, personalized recommendations, and a seamless checkout process, enhancing customer satisfaction.

C. Supply Chain Visibility:

In the retail supply chain, IoT devices enhance visibility by tracking the movement of products from manufacturing to delivery. This transparency improves logistics efficiency, reduces losses, and ensures timely deliveries.

VI. Smart Cities: Creating Connected Urban Environments

A. Intelligent Transportation Systems:

Smart cities integrate IoT into transportation systems for improved traffic management, public transit optimization, and enhanced road safety. Connected vehicles, traffic lights, and sensors contribute to more efficient urban mobility.

B. Environmental Monitoring:

IoT devices in smart cities monitor environmental conditions such as air quality, noise levels, and waste management. This data enables city planners to implement sustainable practices and respond to environmental challenges effectively.

C. Public Safety and Security:

Surveillance cameras, smart streetlights, and connected emergency response systems enhance public safety in smart cities. The ability to collect and analyze data in real-time improves situational awareness and emergency response times.

VII. Challenges and Considerations in IoT Proliferation

A. Security and Privacy Concerns:

The widespread adoption of IoT devices brings forth significant security and privacy challenges. Inadequately secured devices can be vulnerable to cyber-attacks, leading to data breaches and unauthorized access. Ensuring robust security measures and privacy safeguards is paramount.

B. Interoperability:

The diverse array of IoT devices from different manufacturers often operates on different protocols, leading to challenges in interoperability. Standardization efforts are crucial to creating a seamless and interconnected IoT ecosystem.

C. Data Management and Storage:

The immense volume of data generated by IoT devices necessitates efficient data management and storage solutions. Cloud computing and edge computing play vital roles in handling and processing IoT-generated data.

D. Regulatory Compliance:

As IoT devices become integral to various sectors, regulatory frameworks must evolve to address concerns related to security, privacy, and data protection. Compliance with existing and emerging regulations is essential for responsible and ethical IoT deployments.

VIII. Future Trends and Innovations

A. Edge Computing:

The integration of edge computing with IoT is poised to revolutionize data processing. By processing data closer to the source (at the edge), latency is reduced, and real-time insights can be gained, opening new possibilities for IoT applications.

B. 5G Connectivity:

The rollout of 5G networks promises to enhance the connectivity and capabilities of IoT devices. Faster and more reliable communication will drive innovations in IoT applications, particularly in sectors that require low latency and high bandwidth.

C. Artificial Intelligence and Machine Learning:

The synergy between IoT and artificial intelligence (AI) is unlocking advanced capabilities. AI and machine learning algorithms analyze vast datasets from IoT devices, providing predictive insights, anomaly detection, and automation of decision-making processes.

IX. Conclusion: Navigating the IoT Landscape

In conclusion, the proliferation of IoT devices across various sectors marks a paradigm shift in how we interact with and perceive the world. From redefining our living spaces to revolutionizing entire industries, the impact of IoT is profound. However, as we embrace the opportunities presented by IoT, it is crucial to address the associated challenges, particularly in terms of security, privacy, and regulatory compliance.

Navigating the IoT landscape requires a holistic approach that considers the unique requirements of each sector. Standardization, security best practices, and ongoing innovation will be instrumental in unlocking the full potential of IoT while ensuring a secure and interconnected future. As we continue to witness the evolution of IoT technologies, it is imperative to approach the proliferation of devices with a strategic and responsible mindset, acknowledging the transformative power of IoT while safeguarding the principles of security, privacy, and ethical deployment.

The security implications associated with the interconnected nature of IoT.

The interconnected nature of the Internet of Things (IoT) has ushered in a new era of innovation, efficiency, and convenience. However, this interconnectedness is a double-edged sword, presenting a myriad of security challenges that must be addressed to harness the full potential of IoT technologies. In this in-depth exploration, we will delve into the security implications associated with the interconnected nature of IoT, examining the unique vulnerabilities, privacy concerns, and potential threats that arise when devices communicate and collaborate within this expansive ecosystem.

I. The Essence of Interconnected IoT

A. Interdevice Communication:

At the heart of the IoT lies the ability of devices to communicate seamlessly with each other. This interconnectedness allows for a dynamic exchange of data, enabling devices to collaborate, share information, and collectively contribute to the overarching goals of the IoT ecosystem.

B. Collaborative Decision-Making:

Interconnected IoT devices often engage in collaborative decision-making processes. For example, in a smart home environment, sensors in various devices may collectively determine optimal temperature settings based on user preferences, weather conditions, and energy efficiency considerations. This collaborative decision-making is a hallmark of the interconnected IoT landscape.

C. Real-Time Responsiveness:

The interconnected nature of IoT enables real-time responsiveness. Devices can react instantaneously to changes in their environment or inputs from other devices, facilitating adaptive and context-aware functionalities. This real-time responsiveness enhances user experiences but introduces intricate security challenges.

II. Vulnerabilities in the Interconnected IoT Landscape

A. Inadequate Device Authentication:

One of the primary security concerns in interconnected IoT ecosystems is inadequate device authentication. With numerous devices interacting, ensuring the identity and legitimacy of each device becomes a complex challenge. Weak authentication mechanisms can lead to unauthorized access, device spoofing, and malicious infiltration.

B. Insufficient Encryption Protocols:

The data exchanged between interconnected IoT devices is often sensitive and personal. Insufficient or improperly implemented encryption protocols can expose this data to eavesdropping, tampering, or unauthorized access. Strengthening encryption is crucial to preserving the confidentiality and integrity of IoT communications.

C. Proliferation of Legacy Devices:

The IoT landscape includes a diverse range of devices, many of which may be legacy devices lacking modern security features. These devices, if not properly secured, can serve as entry points for attackers to compromise the entire network. The challenge lies in securing both new and existing devices to maintain a robust security posture.

D. Lack of Standardization:

The absence of standardized security protocols across IoT devices contributes to vulnerabilities. Varied implementations of security measures make it challenging to establish a unified and comprehensive security framework. Standardization efforts are essential to create a baseline of security across the interconnected IoT landscape.

III. Privacy Concerns in Interconnected IoT Environments

A. Data Proliferation and Aggregation:

The interconnected nature of IoT results in a vast proliferation of data. As devices communicate and share information, the aggregation of data from multiple sources becomes a privacy concern. Users may be unaware of the extent to which their data is collected, shared, and used for various purposes.

B. Cross-Device Tracking:

Interconnected IoT devices may engage in cross-device tracking to provide personalized experiences. However, this practice raises privacy concerns as it involves monitoring and analyzing user behavior across multiple devices. Striking a balance between personalization and user privacy becomes a crucial consideration.

C. Third-Party Access:

Many interconnected IoT ecosystems involve third-party services or applications. Granting access to these entities introduces potential privacy risks, as users may lose control over the dissemination of their data. Transparent consent mechanisms and robust access controls are essential to mitigate these privacy concerns.

D. User Profiling and Behavioral Analysis:

The interconnectedness of IoT devices enables the creation of detailed user profiles through behavioral analysis. While this data can enhance personalized services, it also raises ethical and privacy considerations. Implementing anonymization techniques and giving users control over their data can help address these concerns.

IV. Threats in the Interconnected IoT Landscape

A. Malware and Botnets:

The interconnected nature of IoT devices makes them susceptible to malware and botnet attacks.

Compromised devices can be enlisted into botnets, leveraging their collective computing power for malicious activities such as Distributed Denial of Service (DDoS) attacks or unauthorized data access.

B. Man-in-the-Middle Attacks:

Interdevice communication in IoT ecosystems creates opportunities for man-in-the-middle attacks. Attackers can intercept and manipulate data exchanges between devices, leading to unauthorized control, data manipulation, or injection of malicious code into the communication stream.

C. Device Tampering and Manipulation:

The interconnectedness of devices creates a potential attack surface for physical tampering. Attackers may attempt to manipulate sensors, actuators, or communication channels to disrupt device functionality, deceive other devices, or compromise the integrity of data.

D. Insider Threats:

Within interconnected IoT ecosystems, insider threats can have significant consequences. Authorized devices with compromised security credentials or malicious intent can exploit their interconnected status to compromise other devices and the overall system.

V. Mitigation Strategies for Interconnected IoT Security

A. Robust Authentication Mechanisms:

Implementing robust authentication mechanisms is crucial for verifying the identity of interconnected IoT devices. Techniques such as biometric authentication, multi-factor authentication, and secure key management enhance the security posture of the ecosystem.

B. End-to-End Encryption:

Employing end-to-end encryption ensures that data exchanged between interconnected devices remains confidential and secure. Strong encryption algorithms and regular updates to encryption protocols are essential to mitigate the risk of unauthorized access.

C. Regular Software Updates:

Frequent software updates, including security patches, are vital for addressing vulnerabilities in IoT devices. Automated update mechanisms can help ensure that devices remain resilient to emerging threats and that security patches are promptly applied.

D. Security-by-Design Principles:

Adopting security-by-design principles involves integrating security measures throughout the entire lifecycle of IoT devices. This proactive approach considers security aspects from the initial design phase to deployment and regular maintenance, reducing the likelihood of vulnerabilities.

E. Network Segmentation:

Implementing network segmentation within interconnected IoT environments helps contain potential security breaches. Segregating devices based on functionality or security levels prevents lateral movement of attackers within the network.

F. Privacy-Enhancing Technologies:

Incorporating privacy-enhancing technologies, such as differential privacy and homomorphic encryption, can safeguard user data in interconnected IoT ecosystems. These technologies enable data analysis without compromising individual privacy.

G. User Education and Awareness:

Raising awareness among users about the security and privacy implications of interconnected IoT devices is crucial. Educated users are more likely to make informed decisions about device permissions, data sharing, and privacy settings.

VI. Standardization Efforts and Regulatory Landscape

A. Industry Standards:

Standardization efforts play a pivotal role in addressing security challenges in the interconnected IoT landscape. Industry consortiums and standards organizations work towards establishing common security frameworks, protocols, and best practices.

B. Regulatory Compliance:

The regulatory landscape for IoT security is evolving globally. Governments and regulatory bodies are recognizing the need for comprehensive guidelines to ensure the security and privacy of interconnected IoT ecosystems. Compliance with these regulations is essential for responsible IoT deployments.

C. Certification Programs:

Certification programs for IoT devices validate their adherence to security standards. Manufacturers participating in certification programs demonstrate their commitment to producing secure and reliable interconnected devices, instilling confidence in consumers and businesses.

VII. The Future of Interconnected IoT Security

A. Artificial Intelligence for Threat Detection:

The integration of artificial intelligence (AI) in IoT security holds promise for advanced threat detection. AI algorithms can analyze vast datasets generated by interconnected devices, identifying patterns indicative of potential security threats and anomalies.

B. Blockchain for Enhanced Security:

Blockchain technology is being explored to enhance the security of interconnected IoT ecosystems. Decentralized and tamper-resistant ledgers can provide secure and transparent transaction histories, mitigating the risk of data manipulation or unauthorized access.

C. Collaborative Security Measures:

As the IoT landscape continues to evolve, collaborative security measures are gaining importance. Information sharing among devices, threat intelligence platforms, and security ecosystems can enhance the collective defense against emerging threats.

VIII. Conclusion: Navigating the Complex Web of Interconnected IoT Security

In conclusion, the interconnected nature of IoT devices offers unparalleled possibilities for innovation and efficiency across diverse sectors. However, to fully harness the transformative potential of interconnected IoT, addressing the associated security implications is imperative. From vulnerabilities and privacy concerns to evolving threats, navigating the complex web of interconnected IoT security requires a multifaceted approach.

By implementing robust authentication mechanisms, prioritizing end-to-end encryption, and embracing security-by-design principles, stakeholders can build resilient IoT ecosystems. Standardization efforts, regulatory compliance, and certification programs contribute to establishing a secure foundation for interconnected IoT deployments.

As we look to the future, the integration of artificial intelligence, blockchain, and collaborative security measures will play pivotal roles in fortifying interconnected IoT ecosystems against emerging threats. Navigating this complex landscape demands continuous innovation, proactive security measures, and a commitment to ensuring the trust and resilience of interconnected IoT devices. In doing so, we can pave the way for a connected future that is not only efficient and innovative but also secure and trustworthy.

2. IoT Device Vulnerabilities

Common vulnerabilities in IoT devices

The proliferation of Internet of Things (IoT) devices has heralded a new era of connectivity and convenience, transforming the way we interact with the world. However, this rapid expansion comes with a downside — a myriad of security vulnerabilities that threaten the integrity, confidentiality, and availability of these interconnected devices. In this exhaustive exploration, we will dissect the common vulnerabilities plaguing IoT devices, unraveling the intricacies of each flaw, and proposing strategies to fortify the security posture of the ever-growing IoT landscape.

I. Inadequate Device Authentication

A. Weak Credential Management:

One of the most pervasive vulnerabilities in IoT devices is weak credential management. Many devices come with default usernames and passwords that are rarely changed by end-users. Attackers exploit this oversight by launching brute-force attacks, easily gaining unauthorized access to the device.

B. Lack of Multi-Factor Authentication:

The absence of multi-factor authentication (MFA) exacerbates the vulnerability of IoT devices. Implementing MFA adds an additional layer of security, requiring users to provide multiple forms of identification before accessing the device. Devices lacking this safeguard are more susceptible to unauthorized access.

C. Insecure Key Management:

Insecure key management practices in IoT devices can lead to compromised cryptographic keys. Weak key generation, inadequate storage, or improper handling of keys expose encrypted communications to potential exploitation, jeopardizing the confidentiality of data exchanged between devices.

II. Insufficient Encryption Protocols

A. Lack of Transport Layer Security (TLS):

Inadequate implementation of Transport Layer Security (TLS) is a prevalent vulnerability in IoT devices. Without proper TLS configurations, data transmitted between devices can be intercepted, tampered with, or eavesdropped on by malicious actors, compromising the confidentiality and integrity of communications.

B. Use of Outdated Encryption Algorithms:

Some IoT devices employ outdated or insecure encryption algorithms, rendering them susceptible to cryptographic attacks. Attackers leverage advancements in computational power to exploit vulnerabilities in obsolete algorithms, decrypting sensitive information and compromising device security.

C. Failure to Encrypt Stored Data:

IoT devices often store sensitive data, such as user credentials or configuration settings, without encryption. In the event of unauthorized access or device compromise, unencrypted stored data becomes an easy target, leading to potential data breaches and privacy violations.

III. Proliferation of Legacy Devices

A. Lack of Security Updates:

Legacy IoT devices, characterized by outdated hardware or firmware, often lack support for security updates. Manufacturers may discontinue support for these devices, leaving them vulnerable to known exploits that remain unaddressed, creating a perpetual security risk.

B. Inability to Implement Modern Security Measures:

Legacy devices may lack the computational power or memory required to implement modern security measures. This limitation hinders the deployment of robust security protocols, leaving the devices susceptible to a wide range of cyber threats.

C. Absence of Security-by-Design Principles:

Many legacy IoT devices were not designed with security in mind. The absence of security-by-design principles during the development phase results in inherent vulnerabilities that persist throughout the device's lifecycle.

IV. Lack of Standardization

A. Diverse Implementation of Security Measures:

The absence of standardized security protocols across IoT devices contributes to vulnerabilities. Varying implementations of security measures make it challenging to establish a unified and comprehensive security framework, leaving devices susceptible to exploits.

B. Interoperability Challenges:

IoT ecosystems consist of devices from different manufacturers, each potentially employing distinct security standards. Interoperability challenges arise when devices need to communicate securely across diverse protocols, leading to potential vulnerabilities in the communication channels.

C. Limited Oversight in Device Development:

A lack of standardized security guidelines can result in limited oversight during the development of IoT devices. Manufacturers may neglect crucial security considerations, inadvertently introducing vulnerabilities that could have been mitigated with a standardized framework.

V. Insecure Network Connections

A. Lack of Secure Bootstrapping:

Securely establishing initial communication between IoT devices, known as bootstrapping, is critical for overall security. Insecure bootstrapping methods may expose devices to man-in-the-middle attacks or unauthorized access during the initiation of communication.

B. Weaknesses in Wi-Fi and Bluetooth Protocols:

IoT devices often rely on wireless communication protocols such as Wi-Fi or Bluetooth. Weaknesses in these protocols, such as insufficient encryption or susceptibility to jamming attacks, expose devices to potential compromise and unauthorized access.

C. Inadequate Network Segmentation:

The absence of network segmentation within IoT ecosystems can facilitate lateral movement for attackers. Segregating devices based on functionality or security levels helps contain potential security breaches, preventing attackers from moving freely within the network.

VI. Insufficient Physical Security Measures

A. Lack of Tamper Detection:

Physical tampering with IoT devices poses a significant threat. The absence of tamper detection mechanisms allows attackers to manipulate the device's hardware, potentially compromising its functionality, extracting sensitive information, or injecting malicious code.

B. Insecure Device Installation:

During device installation, inadequate security measures can expose IoT devices to physical attacks. Devices that are easily accessible or lack protective enclosures may be vulnerable to tampering, unauthorized access, or theft.

C. Weaknesses in Supply Chain Security:

Compromised supply chain security can introduce vulnerabilities at the manufacturing or distribution stages. Insecure supply chains may result in the inclusion of malicious components, firmware, or software in IoT devices, compromising their integrity and security.

VII. Lack of User Awareness and Education

A. Inadequate User Guidance:

Users of IoT devices may not be adequately informed about security best practices. Inadequate user guidance can lead to poor security hygiene, such as using weak passwords, neglecting software updates, or overlooking the importance of configuring security settings.

B. Limited Transparency in Data Practices:

Users may be unaware of how their data is collected, processed, and shared by IoT devices. Limited transparency in data practices can contribute to privacy concerns and erode user trust in the security of the devices they use.

C. Complexity of Security Settings:

Complicated security settings and configurations may discourage users from implementing necessary security measures. User-friendly interfaces and clear instructions are essential to empower users to take proactive steps in securing their IoT devices.

VIII. Strategies for Mitigating IoT Device Vulnerabilities

A. Robust Authentication Mechanisms:

Implementing robust authentication mechanisms, including multi-factor authentication, strengthens the security of IoT devices by verifying the identity of users and devices.

B. Regular Software Updates:

Frequent software updates, including security patches, are crucial for addressing vulnerabilities and ensuring that IoT devices remain resilient to emerging threats.

C. Security-by-Design Principles:

Incorporating security-by-design principles throughout the entire lifecycle of IoT devices helps identify and address vulnerabilities from the initial design phase to deployment and maintenance.

D. Encryption Best Practices:

Adopting encryption best practices, such as using modern algorithms, encrypting both data in transit and at rest, and securely managing cryptographic keys, enhances the confidentiality and integrity of IoT communications.

E. Standardization Efforts:

Supporting and participating in standardization efforts within the IoT industry contributes to the establishment of common security frameworks, protocols, and best practices.

F. User Education and Awareness:

Raising awareness among users about security best practices, the importance of regular updates, and the potential risks associated with IoT devices empowers users to make informed decisions.

G. Supply Chain Security:

Ensuring robust supply chain security practices, such as secure sourcing, rigorous testing, and verification of components, prevents the introduction of compromised elements into IoT devices.

IX. Conclusion: Safeguarding the IoT Ecosystem

In conclusion, the vulnerabilities inherent in IoT devices demand a comprehensive and collaborative approach to mitigate the risks. From inadequate authentication to insecure network connections, addressing these vulnerabilities requires a concerted effort from manufacturers, developers, regulators, and end-users.

As the IoT landscape continues to evolve, the adoption of best practices, adherence to security standards, and the integration of security measures at every stage of device development are imperative. Only through a collective commitment to security and resilience can we navigate the complexities of the IoT ecosystem and unlock its full potential while safeguarding the privacy and security of users worldwide.

The security risks posed by insecure firmware, weak authentication, and lack of encryption

In the ever-expanding realm of the Internet of Things (IoT), the triumvirate of insecure firmware, weak authentication, and lack of encryption stands as a formidable challenge to the security and integrity of connected devices. This comprehensive exploration will dissect the technical intricacies of these security risks, unraveling the potential threats they pose to IoT ecosystems. By delving into the technical aspects of each risk, we aim to provide a nuanced understanding of the vulnerabilities and propose strategies for fortification.

I. Insecure Firmware: A Breeding Ground for Exploits
A. Vulnerabilities in Firmware Code:

The firmware of IoT devices serves as the bridge between hardware and software, enabling device functionality. Insecure firmware arises from vulnerabilities in the code, such as buffer overflows, injection flaws, or insufficient input validation. Attackers exploit these vulnerabilities to inject malicious code, compromising the entire device.

B. Lack of Secure Boot Processes:

Secure boot processes are fundamental to ensuring the integrity of firmware. Without robust measures in place, attackers can manipulate the boot process, loading unauthorized or malicious firmware. This undermines the device's trustworthiness and opens the door to various security threats.

C. Outdated Firmware and Patch Management:

Devices with outdated firmware versions often lack critical security patches, exposing them to known vulnerabilities. Insecure patch management processes can further exacerbate the problem, as delays in updating firmware leave devices susceptible to exploitation.

II. Weak Authentication: Gateway to Unauthorized Access

A. Default Credentials and Credential Stuffing:

IoT devices frequently ship with default usernames and passwords, creating a significant vulnerability. Attackers exploit these defaults through credential stuffing attacks, where they systematically attempt known combinations to gain unauthorized access. Weak, easily guessable passwords compound this issue.

B. Lack of Multi-Factor Authentication (MFA):

Multi-Factor Authentication (MFA) adds an additional layer of security by requiring users to provide multiple forms of identification. The absence of MFA leaves devices vulnerable to unauthorized access, especially when attackers obtain or brute-force login credentials.

C. Insecure Session Management:

Insecure session management practices can lead to session hijacking or session fixation attacks. Weak session tokens, improper timeout settings, or insufficient protection against session replay attacks expose IoT devices to the risk of unauthorized control.

III. Lack of Encryption: Unveiling Sensitive Data to Prying Eyes

A. Insecure Data in Transit:

The lack of encryption for data in transit leaves communications between IoT devices vulnerable to interception and tampering. Attackers can exploit unencrypted channels to eavesdrop on sensitive information, leading to potential data breaches and unauthorized access.

B. Unprotected Data at Rest:

Failure to encrypt data stored on IoT devices poses a significant risk. In the event of physical access or device compromise, unencrypted stored data becomes an easy target for unauthorized extraction, potentially exposing sensitive information or compromising user privacy.

C. Weak Key Management:

Effective encryption relies on robust key management practices. Weaknesses in key generation, storage, or distribution can compromise the confidentiality of encrypted data. Attackers may exploit vulnerabilities in key management to decrypt sensitive information and manipulate device communications.

IV. Technical Strategies for Mitigating Insecure Firmware, Weak Authentication, and Lack of Encryption

A. Secure Firmware Development Lifecycle:
Code Review and Analysis:

Conduct thorough code reviews and static analysis to identify and remediate vulnerabilities in firmware code. Automated tools and manual inspections play crucial roles in this process.

Secure Boot Processes:

Implement secure boot processes that verify the integrity of firmware during device startup. This involves using cryptographic signatures and secure storage mechanisms to ensure that only authenticated and unmodified firmware is executed.

Firmware Signing and Validation:

Employ digital signatures to sign firmware images, and validate these signatures during the boot process. This ensures the authenticity and integrity of the firmware, preventing unauthorized modifications.

Timely Patch Management:

Establish a robust and timely patch management process to address vulnerabilities promptly. Regularly update firmware with security patches to mitigate known risks and enhance the overall security posture.

B. Strengthening Authentication Mechanisms:
Eliminate Default Credentials:

Manufacturers should eliminate default usernames and passwords, forcing users to set unique credentials during the initial setup. This reduces the attack surface by removing the predictability associated with default credentials.

Enforce Strong Password Policies:

Implement and enforce strong password policies, requiring users to create complex passwords. This includes setting minimum length requirements, mandating the use of alphanumeric characters, and enforcing regular password changes.

Multi-Factor Authentication (MFA):

Integrate MFA into the authentication process to add an additional layer of security. This may involve the use of one-time codes, biometric authentication, or token-based authentication methods.

Secure Session Management:

Implement secure session management practices, including the use of secure session tokens, proper timeout settings, and protection against session-related attacks. Regularly rotate session keys to minimize the risk of compromise.

C. Robust Encryption Practices:

End-to-End Encryption:

Implement end-to-end encryption to protect data transmitted between IoT devices. This ensures that even if intercepted, the data remains confidential and integral throughout the communication process.

Data-at-Rest Encryption:

Utilize strong encryption algorithms to protect data stored on IoT devices. Encrypt sensitive information such as user credentials, configuration settings, and other pertinent data to prevent unauthorized access in the event of a security breach.

Key Management Best Practices:

Adhere to key management best practices, including the secure generation, storage, and distribution of cryptographic keys. Regularly rotate keys, use hardware-based key storage solutions, and implement secure key exchange mechanisms.

41

Use of Secure Protocols:

Ensure that IoT devices communicate using secure and updated communication protocols. Utilize protocols such as TLS for secure data transmission, and regularly update to newer versions to benefit from the latest security enhancements.

V. Conclusion: Securing the Foundation of IoT Devices

In conclusion, addressing the security risks posed by insecure firmware, weak authentication, and lack of encryption requires a multifaceted approach grounded in technical strategies. Manufacturers, developers, and security professionals must collaborate to fortify the foundation of IoT devices, ensuring that they not only provide unparalleled connectivity and functionality but also uphold the principles of security and privacy.

By embracing secure development practices, strengthening authentication mechanisms, and implementing robust encryption measures, the IoT ecosystem can evolve into a secure and resilient landscape. As the interconnectivity of devices continues to shape the future, the technical fortification of IoT devices becomes paramount, safeguarding users, data, and the integrity of the interconnected world we inhabit.

Examples of real-world IoT security breaches

There are many examples that underscore the diverse range of IoT security breaches, from massive DDoS attacks leveraging compromised devices to vulnerabilities in medical implants and concerns about the privacy of connected toys. They highlight the importance of addressing security challenges in the rapidly expanding IoT landscape.

Mirai Botnet (2016):

● Description: The Mirai botnet is one of the most infamous IoT-related security incidents. It targeted and compromised a large number of IoT devices, primarily routers and cameras, by exploiting default usernames and passwords.

● Impact: Mirai enslaved these devices, turning them into a massive botnet. The botnet was then used to launch powerful Distributed Denial of Service (DDoS) attacks, causing widespread internet disruptions, including the notable attack on Dyn DNS, which affected major websites like Twitter, Netflix, and Reddit.

St. Jude Medical Cardiac Devices (2017):

● Description: Vulnerabilities were discovered in St. Jude Medical's implantable cardiac devices, including pacemakers and defibrillators. These vulnerabilities could potentially allow attackers to remotely control the devices.

● Impact: Although there were no known instances of real-world harm, the discovery raised concerns about the security of medical IoT devices and highlighted the potential risks associated with compromised healthcare technology.

WannaCry Ransomware (2017):

● Description: While not exclusively an IoT breach, the WannaCry ransomware targeted a vulnerability in Microsoft Windows that was prevalent in many IoT devices. The ransomware spread rapidly across networks, impacting various industries.

● Impact: Hospitals, factories, and other critical infrastructure were affected. The incident underscored the interconnected nature of IT and OT (Operational Technology) systems and the potential for ransomware to disrupt a wide range of IoT devices.

Dynacolor Camera Vulnerabilities (2017):

● Description: Security researchers identified vulnerabilities in certain Dynacolor camera models that allowed unauthorized users to access the devices and view live camera feeds.

● Impact: The vulnerabilities raised concerns about the privacy and security of IoT devices, especially those used in surveillance. The incident highlighted the importance of manufacturers addressing security issues in their products.

My Friend Cayla Doll (2017):

● Description: The My Friend Cayla doll, equipped with IoT capabilities, was found to have vulnerabilities that could potentially allow malicious actors to eavesdrop on conversations and engage in unauthorized data collection.

● Impact: This breach emphasized the need for stringent security measures in IoT devices designed for children. It led to increased scrutiny of smart toys and their potential privacy implications.

NotPetya Ransomware (2017):

● Description: NotPetya, similar to WannaCry, exploited a vulnerability in Microsoft Windows, affecting various systems, including IoT devices. The malware spread rapidly, encrypting data and demanding ransom payments.

● Impact: The ransomware caused widespread disruptions, affecting shipping, manufacturing, and critical infrastructure. The incident highlighted the importance of promptly patching and securing IoT devices to prevent large-scale attacks.

VPNFilter Malware (2018):

● Description: VPNFilter was a sophisticated malware that targeted routers and network-attached storage (NAS) devices. It had the capability to collect information, manipulate network traffic, and even render devices unusable.

● Impact: The malware, attributed to a state-sponsored group, raised concerns about the security of network infrastructure. It demonstrated the potential for IoT devices to be targeted for espionage and cyber warfare.

3. Securing IoT Networks

Challenges of securing IoT networks

The proliferation of the Internet of Things (IoT) has ushered in a new era of connectivity, transforming the way devices communicate and share information. While the benefits are immense, the security landscape surrounding IoT networks is rife with challenges that demand nuanced solutions. This exploration delves into the multifaceted challenges posed by securing IoT networks, offering insights into the intricate interplay of technology, user behavior, and evolving threats.

The Heterogeneity Dilemma

In the realm of IoT, diversity is both a strength and a challenge. The heterogeneous nature of devices—from simple sensors to complex industrial machinery—introduces a unique set of security considerations. Each device comes with its own communication protocols, hardware capabilities, and security postures, making the task of securing such a diverse ecosystem complex and multifaceted.

Resource Constraints and Security Trade-offs

IoT devices often operate with limited resources, including processing power, memory, and energy. The challenge lies in implementing effective security measures without compromising the functionality of these resource-constrained devices. Striking the right balance requires innovative approaches that leverage lightweight security protocols and efficient resource management.

Retrofitting Security: A Historical Oversight

In the rush to bring IoT devices to market, security considerations were often relegated to a secondary role.

Many devices were not designed with security as a primary focus. Retrofitting security into existing devices poses a significant challenge, necessitating a paradigm shift in the industry toward prioritizing security from the inception of new IoT designs.

The Interoperability Quandary

Interoperability, a cornerstone of IoT's potential, becomes a double-edged sword when it comes to security. Devices from different manufacturers may employ disparate communication protocols and security standards, hindering the establishment of a cohesive and standardized security framework across the entire network. Bridging this interoperability gap is crucial for holistic security.

Authentication: The Gateway to Security

Robust authentication mechanisms are paramount in the sprawling landscape of IoT networks. Yet, many devices still rely on weak or default credentials, leaving networks vulnerable to unauthorized access, data breaches, and potential manipulation of devices. Strengthening authentication across the ecosystem is imperative for a secure IoT environment.

Encryption: Safeguarding Data in Transit and at Rest

Ensuring the confidentiality and integrity of data transmitted within IoT networks is a critical concern. Resource constraints often hinder the implementation of strong encryption protocols, creating opportunities for attackers to intercept and manipulate sensitive information. Overcoming these challenges requires innovative encryption solutions that align with the limitations of IoT devices.

Over-the-Air (OTA) Updates: A Patchwork of Challenges

Maintaining the security of IoT devices over their lifecycle demands timely software updates. However, the absence of standardized over-the-air (OTA) update mechanisms poses challenges. This limitation leaves devices unpatched and susceptible to known vulnerabilities, especially in scenarios where physical access for manual updates is impractical.

Complexity Amplified: Navigating Network Architecture

The complexity of IoT network architectures, spanning edge computing, cloud services, and multiple communication layers, introduces challenges in monitoring, management, and enforcement of security policies. The dynamic nature of IoT environments requires adaptive security solutions capable of addressing the evolving threat landscape.

Regulatory Gaps: A Call for Universal Standards

The absence of comprehensive regulatory frameworks for IoT security exacerbates challenges. While various industry standards exist, the lack of universal regulations leaves room for inconsistent security practices. A harmonized regulatory approach could establish a baseline for security requirements, fostering a more secure IoT ecosystem.

The Shifting Threat Landscape

As IoT adoption proliferates, the threat landscape continually evolves. Sophisticated cyber threats targeting IoT devices, including ransomware, distributed denial of service (DDoS) attacks, and zero-day exploits, are on the rise. Securing IoT networks necessitates not only addressing current threats but also preparing for emerging risks.

Human Element: A Critical Piece of the Puzzle

Human factors, including end-user behavior and awareness, play a pivotal role in IoT security. Inadequate user awareness, poor password practices, and susceptibility to social engineering attacks contribute to the vulnerability of IoT networks. Effective security strategies must encompass user education and awareness programs to mitigate these risks.

Physical Vulnerabilities: Beyond the Digital Realm

Many IoT devices operate in the physical world, making them susceptible to physical attacks, tampering, and theft. Securing against these physical vulnerabilities requires a combination of robust access controls, tamper-evident designs, and, in some cases, additional physical security measures.

Emerging Technologies: A Double-Edged Sword

The integration of emerging technologies, such as Artificial Intelligence (AI) and blockchain, into IoT networks introduces both opportunities and challenges. While these technologies can enhance security, their integration requires careful consideration of interoperability, performance impact, and potential new attack vectors.

Post-Compromise Strategies: Beyond Prevention

Traditional security measures often focus on preventing breaches, but determined attackers may find ways to compromise IoT networks. The lack of effective post-compromise detection and response mechanisms leaves organizations vulnerable to prolonged undetected attacks, emphasizing the need for continuous monitoring and incident response capabilities.

Vendor and Supply Chain Risks: Guarding the Entry Points

The global nature of IoT supply chains introduces risks related to the security practices of vendors and suppliers. Compromised components, malicious firmware updates, or supply chain attacks can have cascading effects on the security of IoT networks, emphasizing the importance of comprehensive supply chain security measures.

Holistic Recommendations: Fortifying IoT Networks

Addressing these challenges requires a holistic and adaptive approach to IoT network security. Security by design, standardization, user education, regulatory frameworks, and collaborative defense form the pillars of a multifaceted strategy aimed at fortifying IoT networks against evolving threats and vulnerabilities.

The role of firewalls, intrusion detection systems, and network segmentation in IoT security

In the complex landscape of IoT security, where diverse devices interconnect to form expansive networks, the role of robust defense mechanisms is paramount. This exploration delves into the technical aspects of three key components—firewalls, intrusion detection systems (IDS), and network segmentation—and their symbiotic role in fortifying IoT ecosystems against evolving threats.

I. Firewalls: Safeguarding the Perimeter

Overview:

Firewalls stand as the first line of defense, acting as sentinels at the perimeter of IoT networks. Their primary function is to regulate incoming and outgoing network traffic based on predetermined security rules. In the IoT context, firewalls play a pivotal role in controlling communication flows between devices, ensuring that only authorized and secure connections are established.

Key Functions:

1. Packet Filtering:

- Firewalls employ packet filtering to scrutinize data packets entering or leaving the network. This involves inspecting packet headers and making decisions based on predefined rules.

2. Stateful Inspection:

- Stateful inspection adds an intelligent layer to packet filtering, allowing firewalls to analyze the state of active connections. This enables the firewall to make context-aware decisions and thwart malicious activities.

3. Proxying and Network Address Translation (NAT):

- Firewalls often act as intermediaries, employing proxy services to handle communication between internal and external devices. NAT further enhances security by masking internal device IP addresses, adding an additional layer of obscurity.

4. Deep Packet Inspection (DPI):

- DPI involves analyzing the content of data packets beyond headers, enabling firewalls to detect and block malicious payloads. In IoT, DPI becomes crucial in identifying anomalous behavior within device communication.

Challenges and Innovations:

1. IoT Protocol Support:

- Adapting firewalls to support diverse IoT protocols poses a challenge. Modern firewalls are evolving to recognize and interpret IoT-specific protocols, ensuring comprehensive protection.

2. Resource Optimization:

- Resource constraints on some IoT devices necessitate optimized firewall configurations. Innovations include lightweight firewall implementations tailored for IoT environments.

II. Intrusion Detection Systems (IDS): Vigilant Guardians

Overview:

While firewalls establish a barricade at the perimeter, intrusion detection systems (IDS) serve as vigilant guardians within the network. IDS monitors and analyzes internal traffic, identifying patterns indicative of malicious activities or potential security breaches. In the dynamic landscape of IoT, where threats evolve rapidly, IDS plays a critical role in real-time threat detection.

Key Functions:

1. Anomaly Detection:

- IDS utilizes machine learning algorithms to establish baseline behavior for IoT devices. Deviations from these baselines trigger alerts, enabling rapid response to anomalous activities.

2. Signature-Based Detection:

- Signature-based detection involves matching patterns in network traffic against a database of known threat signatures. IDS employs this technique to identify well-established threats within IoT environments.

3. Behavioral Analysis:

- Behavioral analysis examines the conduct of devices over time. Suspicious deviations, such as a sudden surge in data transmission or unauthorized access attempts, prompt immediate intervention.

4. Real-time Alerts:

- IDS generates real-time alerts, notifying security personnel of potential threats. In the context of IoT, where prompt action is imperative, these alerts facilitate swift response and mitigation.

Challenges and Innovations:

1. Scalability:

• The sheer volume of IoT devices necessitates scalable IDS solutions. Innovations focus on distributed architectures and cloud-based IDS deployments to accommodate the scalability requirements of IoT networks.

2. Protocol Diversity:

• IoT devices communicate using diverse protocols. IDS innovations include protocol-agnostic detection mechanisms, ensuring comprehensive coverage across varied communication standards.

III. Network Segmentation: Boundaries of Security

Overview:

Network segmentation involves dividing an IoT network into distinct segments or subnetworks, restricting communication between these segments. This strategy enhances security by containing potential threats, limiting lateral movement in case of a breach, and facilitating granular control over device communication.

Key Functions:

1. Isolation of Critical Assets:

• Critical IoT assets, such as control systems or sensitive data repositories, can be isolated within specific segments. This containment prevents the propagation of threats to vital components.

2. Traffic Control and Prioritization:

• Segmentation allows for fine-grained control over traffic flow between IoT devices. Prioritizing traffic based on device criticality ensures that essential communication pathways remain unhindered.

3. Compartmentalization of Device Types:

- Devices with similar functionalities or security postures can be grouped into segments, streamlining security policies and facilitating targeted monitoring.

Challenges and Innovations:

1. Dynamic Segmentation:

- The dynamic nature of IoT requires adaptive segmentation. Innovations include automated segmentation based on real-time device behavior and threat intelligence, ensuring agility in response to evolving threats.

2. Policy Orchestration:

- Orchestrating segmentation policies for a multitude of devices poses challenges. Innovations involve centralized policy management, leveraging software-defined networking (SDN) principles for efficient and dynamic policy enforcement.

Best practices for safeguarding communication between IoT devices

In the rapidly evolving landscape of the Internet of Things (IoT), where devices communicate seamlessly to enable a myriad of applications, ensuring the security of these communications is paramount. Implementing robust security measures is essential to guarantee the integrity, confidentiality, and availability of the data exchanged between IoT devices. This comprehensive exploration delves into the intricacies of the best practices for securing communication in IoT environments.

1. Encryption Protocols

Implementing strong encryption protocols forms the cornerstone of securing communication between IoT devices. End-to-end encryption ensures that data is encrypted at the source and decrypted only at the intended destination. Commonly used protocols such as TLS (Transport Layer Security) and DTLS (Datagram Transport Layer Security) establish secure communication channels, thwarting eavesdropping and tampering attempts.

2. Authentication Mechanisms

Robust authentication mechanisms are crucial in preventing unauthorized access to IoT devices and the sensitive data they transmit. Device authentication, utilizing methods such as digital certificates or secure tokens, ensures that only authenticated and authorized devices can participate in communication. Mutual authentication further enhances security by verifying the identity of both communicating entities.

3. Secure Key Management

Effective key management is fundamental to maintaining the security of encrypted communication. Safely storing and managing cryptographic keys prevents unauthorized access. Implementing key rotation and ensuring the use of strong, randomly generated keys enhances the overall resilience of the cryptographic infrastructure.

4. Device Identity Management

Assigning unique and immutable identities to IoT devices facilitates secure communication. Device identity management aids in tracking and validating the authenticity of devices within the network. It also enables efficient management of device-specific security policies.

5. Secure Boot Processes

Ensuring the integrity of the boot process is critical for establishing a trusted foundation for IoT devices. Secure boot processes verify the authenticity and integrity of the device firmware and software during startup, mitigating the risk of compromised devices from the outset.

6. Use of Virtual Private Networks (VPNs)

Implementing Virtual Private Networks provides an additional layer of security for IoT communication. VPNs create encrypted tunnels over public networks, securing data in transit between devices. This is particularly beneficial for IoT deployments that span geographically dispersed locations.

7. Regular Software Updates and Patch Management

Keeping IoT device software up-to-date is essential for addressing known vulnerabilities. Regular software updates and patch management practices ensure that devices are equipped with the latest security enhancements, reducing the risk of exploitation.

8. Network Segmentation

Segmenting the IoT network into isolated zones based on device functionalities enhances security. Network segmentation limits lateral movement in the event of a security breach, containing potential threats within specific segments and allowing for more focused monitoring and control.

9. Intrusion Detection and Prevention Systems

Deploying intrusion detection and prevention systems adds an active layer of defense against potential threats. These systems monitor network traffic for anomalous patterns, detect potential security breaches, and take preventive actions to safeguard communication.

10. Data Minimization and Privacy by Design

Adopting a data minimization approach ensures that only essential data is transmitted between IoT devices. Implementing privacy by design principles emphasizes the protection of user privacy, limiting the collection and transmission of sensitive information.

11. Compliance with Industry Standards

Adhering to established industry standards and best practices for IoT security is essential. Compliance with standards such as ISO/IEC 27001, NIST SP 800-53, and the IoT Security Foundation's best practices provides a framework for robust security implementation.

12. Monitoring and Incident Response

Continuous monitoring of IoT network traffic allows for the early detection of security incidents. Establishing a well-defined incident response plan ensures swift and effective responses to security breaches, minimizing potential damage.

In conclusion, safeguarding communication between IoT devices requires a multifaceted approach that encompasses encryption, authentication, secure key management, and adherence to best practices. By implementing these measures, organizations can establish a secure foundation for their IoT deployments, mitigating potential risks and ensuring the resilience of their interconnected ecosystems.

4. Data Privacy in IoT

Address the sensitive nature of data generated by IoT devices

Introduction

The Internet of Things (IoT) has revolutionized the way we interact with the world around us. Every day, more and more devices are being connected to the internet, from our home appliances to our cars, to wearable technology. While this technology brings many conveniences, it also raises significant privacy concerns. The sensitive nature of the data IoT devices collect and transmit is a growing concern in our increasingly interconnected world.

The Nature of Data Collected by IoT Devices

IoT devices collect a wide range of data. A smart thermostat learns your schedule and temperature preferences, a fitness tracker records your physical activity and health metrics, and a smart car collects data about your driving habits and destinations. This data can be incredibly sensitive, as it provides intimate details about your personal life.

For instance, a smart thermostat not only adjusts the temperature of your home but also learns your daily routine. It knows when you're likely to be home, when you're away, and even when you're sleeping. If this information were to fall into the wrong hands, it could be used to determine when your home is likely to be empty, making you a target for burglary.

Similarly, a fitness tracker collects data about your physical activity, heart rate, sleep patterns, and more. This information could reveal sensitive health information that you may not want to be shared. For instance, sudden changes in heart rate or physical activity could indicate a medical condition.

Data Privacy Concerns

The sensitive nature of the data collected by IoT devices raises several privacy concerns:

1.   Unauthorized Access: IoT devices can be hacked, allowing unauthorized individuals to access sensitive data. This could lead to identity theft, financial loss, or even personal harm if the hacked device is a security system or a medical device.

2.   Data Sharing: Many IoT devices transmit the collected data back to the manufacturer or third parties. Users often do not have clear visibility or control over where their data is being sent and how it is being used.

3.   Inadequate Security Measures: Many IoT devices lack robust security measures. Weak passwords, unencrypted data, and outdated software can leave devices vulnerable to attacks.

Addressing Privacy Concerns

Addressing the privacy concerns associated with IoT devices is not a simple task. It requires the combined efforts of manufacturers, legislators, and users. Here are some ways to address these concerns:

1.   Privacy by Design: Manufacturers should incorporate privacy considerations into the design of IoT devices. This includes using strong encryption for data transmission, allowing users to control what data is collected and where it is sent, and regularly updating software to patch vulnerabilities.

2.   Legislation and Regulation: Governments should enact legislation and regulations that protect the privacy of

IoT users. This could include laws that require manufacturers to implement certain security measures, or regulations that limit the types of data that can be collected and how it can be used.

3.   User Awareness and Education: Users must be aware of the privacy risks associated with IoT devices. They should be educated on how to use these devices safely, such as changing default passwords and regularly updating software.

Conclusion

The sensitive nature of the data generated by IoT devices necessitates a proactive approach to privacy. By implementing robust security measures, advocating for protective legislation, and educating users, we can enjoy the benefits of IoT while minimizing privacy risks.

Future Directions

As the IoT continues to grow, it's crucial that privacy remains a top priority. Future research should focus on developing new methods for protecting user data, such as advanced encryption algorithms and machine learning techniques for detecting and preventing unauthorized access. Additionally, policymakers should consider the unique challenges posed by the IoT when drafting privacy legislation. By working together, we can ensure that the IoT brings convenience and innovation without sacrificing privacy.

Privacy concerns related to the collection and storage of IoT data

The Internet of Things (IoT) has revolutionized the way we interact with technology, embedding smart devices in our daily lives. These interconnected devices generate vast amounts of data, offering unprecedented insights into user behavior, preferences, and the surrounding environment. However, this data-driven connectivity raises significant privacy concerns. This essay explores the intricate landscape of privacy issues associated with the collection and storage of IoT data, emphasizing the need for a balanced approach to harness the benefits of IoT while safeguarding individual privacy.

Ubiquitous Data Collection:

One of the primary privacy concerns in the realm of IoT is the ubiquitous collection of data. Smart devices continuously gather information about users, their activities, and their surroundings. From smart home appliances to wearable devices, the sheer volume and granularity of data collected pose a potential threat to individual privacy. Users often unknowingly share sensitive information, such as health metrics, location data, and personal preferences, creating a comprehensive digital profile.

Informed Consent and Transparency:

The issue of informed consent is central to privacy in IoT. Many users are unaware of the extent and nature of data collection by their devices. Manufacturers and service providers must prioritize transparency and ensure that users are fully informed about the data being collected, the purposes for which it is used, and the entities with access to it. Clear and concise privacy policies should be accessible to users, promoting an informed decision-making process.

Security Challenges:

The interconnected nature of IoT devices introduces security challenges that can exacerbate privacy concerns. Weak security measures may lead to unauthorized access, data breaches, and misuse of sensitive information. Insecure IoT devices can be exploited as entry points for cyberattacks, jeopardizing not only user privacy but also the integrity of larger networks. Strengthening security protocols and implementing robust encryption methods are essential in mitigating these risks.

Profiling and Predictive Analytics:

The extensive data collected by IoT devices enables the creation of detailed user profiles. This data can be leveraged for targeted advertising, personalized services, and even predictive analytics. While these applications offer convenience and efficiency, they also raise concerns about the commodification of personal information. Users may feel exposed and vulnerable when their behaviors are predicted, influencing decisions made on their behalf. Striking a balance between personalization and privacy becomes imperative in this context.

Location Tracking and Geospatial Data:

Location tracking is a common feature in many IoT devices, providing valuable data for various applications, such as navigation, emergency services, and location-based recommendations. However, the constant monitoring of an individual's location raises serious privacy issues. Unauthorized access to geospatial data can lead to stalking, unauthorized surveillance, and compromise personal safety. Implementing strict access controls and anonymizing location data are crucial steps in addressing these concerns.

Data Retention and Ownership:

The storage of IoT data poses additional privacy challenges, especially in terms of data retention and ownership. Users may be unaware of how long their data is stored and who retains control over it. Clear data retention policies and mechanisms for users to reclaim control over their data are essential components of a privacy-centric IoT ecosystem. Empowering individuals to manage their data contributes to a sense of agency and control over personal information.

Legal and Regulatory Frameworks:

To address the growing privacy concerns associated with IoT data, legal and regulatory frameworks play a crucial role. Policymakers must adapt to the evolving landscape of IoT, developing legislation that balances innovation and privacy protection. Additionally, international cooperation is essential to harmonize privacy standards and ensure a consistent approach to IoT data protection across borders.

Conclusion:

As the Internet of Things continues to permeate various aspects of our lives, the privacy concerns related to the collection and storage of IoT data demand thoughtful consideration. Balancing the benefits of interconnected devices with the need to safeguard individual privacy requires a collaborative effort from manufacturers, service providers, policymakers, and users. By prioritizing informed consent, transparency, security, and user empowerment, we can navigate the complexities of the digital landscape and foster a privacy-centric approach to IoT development and implementation. Ultimately, achieving this balance is essential for building trust in IoT technologies and harnessing their full potential while respecting individual privacy rights.

Encryption and anonymization techniques to protect user privacy

In the rapidly evolving landscape of the Internet of Things (IoT), where interconnected devices constantly exchange data, ensuring the privacy and security of user information is paramount. This essay delves into the critical role played by encryption and anonymization techniques in fortifying user privacy within the IoT ecosystem. By examining the nuanced applications of these protective measures, we can gain insights into how they collectively contribute to mitigating potential threats, securing sensitive information, and fostering a robust and private IoT environment.

Encryption in IoT. Securing Data in Transit.

Encryption is fundamental to securing data as it traverses the IoT network. The continuous exchange of information between devices and the cloud exposes data to potential interception. Robust encryption algorithms ensure that even if data is intercepted, it remains indecipherable without the appropriate decryption keys. This process is crucial in preventing unauthorized access and safeguarding the confidentiality of sensitive information.

End-to-End Encryption:

End-to-end encryption is a pivotal strategy, particularly in complex IoT networks where data passes through multiple nodes. By encrypting data at the source and maintaining encryption until it reaches its final

destination, end-to-end encryption enhances security. This approach minimizes the points at which data is decrypted, reducing the risk of vulnerabilities within the network.
Device-Level Encryption:

Many IoT devices process and store sensitive data locally. Implementing encryption at the device level adds an extra layer of protection, especially in scenarios where physical tampering or theft is a concern. Device-level encryption ensures that even if a device is compromised, the data stored on it remains secure, preserving the integrity and confidentiality of information.
Anonymization in IoT:
Preserving User Identities:

Anonymization is the process of removing personally identifiable information from data, a critical step in protecting user identities. In the context of IoT, where data often relates to specific users or devices, anonymization becomes imperative. By eliminating identifiable markers, individuals can reap the benefits of IoT services without compromising their privacy.
Dynamic Anonymization Techniques:

Dynamic anonymization techniques go beyond static methods by continually altering or rotating identifiers associated with IoT devices. This approach adds complexity, making it more challenging for malicious entities to track and correlate data over time. Dynamic anonymization enhances resilience against sophisticated attacks seeking to de-anonymize users through prolonged data analysis.
Aggregation and Generalization:

Aggregating and generalizing data involve summarizing or combining information to reduce granularity. By presenting data in a more generalized form, the risk of exposing specific details about individuals or their behaviors is minimized. This approach ensures that valuable insights can be derived from the data while protecting user privacy.

Challenges and Considerations:

Performance Impact:

Encryption and anonymization may introduce performance overhead, especially in resource-constrained IoT devices. Striking a balance between robust security measures and operational efficiency is crucial for seamless IoT ecosystem functioning.

Key Management:

Effective encryption relies on robust key management practices. If encryption keys are compromised, the entire security infrastructure may be at risk. Regular key rotation and secure storage are essential for maintaining encryption integrity in IoT.

Regulatory Compliance:

Navigating diverse privacy regulations is a challenge for IoT developers. Ensuring compliance with regional laws is crucial, emphasizing the importance of privacy by design and default to stay ahead of regulatory requirements.

Conclusion:

As IoT continues to reshape our digital landscape, prioritizing user privacy is essential. Encryption and anonymization techniques emerge as powerful tools in achieving this balance, offering robust solutions to mitigate risks and vulnerabilities. By thoughtfully implementing these measures, IoT developers can create a secure, private, and trustworthy digital ecosystem for the future.

5. IoT Security Standards and Regulations

Overview of existing standards and regulations specific to IoT security

The field of the Internet of Things (IoT) brings forth unprecedented opportunities but also introduces new challenges, particularly in the realm of security. Recognizing the critical importance of safeguarding interconnected devices and systems, various standards and regulations have emerged to establish a framework for IoT security. This comprehensive overview delves into existing standards and regulations specific to IoT security, offering insights into the evolving landscape of compliance and best practices.

1. Introduction

The proliferation of IoT devices has prompted a global response to address the associated security risks. Governments, industry bodies, and international organizations have played pivotal roles in shaping standards and regulations to guide the secure development and deployment of IoT technologies.

2. International Standards

a. ISO/IEC 27001 for Information Security Management Systems

The ISO/IEC 27001 standard provides a foundation for implementing information security management systems. While not IoT-specific, its principles are applicable to IoT deployments. Organizations leveraging IoT technologies can use ISO/IEC 27001 to establish a robust security management framework.

b. ISO/IEC 15408 Common Criteria for Information Technology Security Evaluation

Common Criteria is an international standard for evaluating and certifying the security features of IT products. It ensures that products meet specific security requirements. While not exclusive to IoT, adherence to Common Criteria enhances the overall security posture of IoT devices.

3. Regional Regulations

a. GDPR (General Data Protection Regulation) in the European Union

GDPR, although not IoT-specific, has a profound impact on IoT devices due to their inherent data processing capabilities. It mandates stringent data protection measures, emphasizing user consent, data minimization, and the right to be forgotten. Organizations deploying IoT solutions in the European Union must align with GDPR requirements.

b. NIST Cybersecurity Framework in the United States

The National Institute of Standards and Technology (NIST) Cybersecurity Framework provides a risk-based approach to managing cybersecurity. While not IoT-centric, its principles are applicable to IoT security. The framework offers a set of guidelines and best practices for enhancing the security of connected systems.

4. Industry-specific Standards

a. IEC 62443 for Industrial Control Systems (ICS) Security

IEC 62443 is a series of standards focusing on the cybersecurity of industrial automation and control systems. As industries increasingly adopt IoT technologies, compliance with IEC 62443 ensures the security of critical infrastructure.

b. HIPAA (Health Insurance Portability and Accountability Act) for Healthcare IoT

In the healthcare sector, where IoT plays a pivotal role, adherence to HIPAA is essential. HIPAA sets forth regulations for safeguarding protected health information (PHI), imposing strict controls on the collection, storage, and transmission of health data through IoT devices.

5. IoT-specific Standards

a. IoT Security Foundation Best Practices

The IoT Security Foundation provides a set of best practices specifically tailored for IoT deployments. These guidelines cover various aspects, including device provisioning, secure coding, and incident response. Adhering to these best practices enhances the overall security posture of IoT ecosystems.

b. OWASP IoT Top Ten

The Open Web Application Security Project (OWASP) IoT Top Ten outlines the most critical security risks facing IoT systems. It serves as a valuable resource for developers and organizations to prioritize and address common vulnerabilities in IoT deployments.

6. Challenges and Evolving Landscape

While existing standards and regulations provide a foundational framework for IoT security, challenges persist. The dynamic nature of IoT, rapid technological advancements, and diverse use cases pose ongoing challenges for regulators and standardization bodies. Balancing security requirements with the need for innovation remains a delicate endeavor.

7. Future Directions

The landscape of IoT security standards and regulations is expected to evolve in response to emerging threats and technological advancements. Efforts to develop industry-specific standards and harmonize existing frameworks will likely shape the future of IoT security governance.

8. Conclusion

Navigating the complex landscape of IoT security demands a multifaceted approach that encompasses international standards, regional regulations, industry-specific guidelines, and IoT-focused best practices. Compliance with these standards not only mitigates risks but also fosters trust among users, stakeholders, and regulatory bodies, ensuring the responsible and secure evolution of the IoT ecosystem.

This comprehensive overview of existing standards and regulations specific to IoT security provides insights into the multifaceted landscape of compliance, offering guidance for organizations seeking to navigate the complex terrain of securing interconnected devices.

Compliance requirements and the importance of adhering to industry standards

The explosive growth of the Internet of Things (IoT) has ushered in unprecedented connectivity and transformative potential across various industries. However, this connectivity also introduces a plethora of security and privacy challenges. To address these challenges and establish a secure and trustworthy IoT ecosystem, compliance requirements and adherence to industry standards play a pivotal role. This exploration delves into the critical importance of complying with regulatory requirements and industry standards in the IoT landscape.

1. The Regulatory Landscape for IoT

a. GDPR and Data Protection

In the European Union, the General Data Protection Regulation (GDPR) is a cornerstone of data protection. Its implications for IoT are profound, as these devices inherently process vast amounts of personal data. Adherence to GDPR ensures that IoT deployments prioritize user privacy, consent, and transparent data processing practices.

b. HIPAA in Healthcare IoT

For the healthcare sector leveraging IoT, compliance with the Health Insurance Portability and Accountability Act (HIPAA) is non-negotiable. HIPAA safeguards protected health information (PHI), imposing strict controls on how healthcare IoT devices handle, transmit, and store sensitive patient data.

c. FCC Regulations for Spectrum Usage

In the United States, the Federal Communications Commission (FCC) governs the use of radio frequency spectrum. IoT devices often rely on wireless communication, and compliance with FCC regulations ensures interference-free operation and adherence to allocated spectrum bands.

2. Industry-specific Compliance

a. IEC 62443 for Industrial IoT Security

In the realm of industrial IoT (IIoT), compliance with the International Electrotechnical Commission (IEC) 62443 series is essential. These standards address the unique cybersecurity challenges faced by industrial control systems, providing guidelines for securing critical infrastructure.

b. ISO/SAE 21434 for Automotive IoT Security

The automotive industry, embracing IoT for innovations like connected vehicles, adheres to ISO/SAE 21434. This standard outlines cybersecurity engineering processes for the automotive sector, ensuring the security of in-vehicle systems and communications.

3. Importance of IoT Industry Standards

a. Security-by-Design Principles

Adhering to industry standards fosters a "security by design" approach, integrating security measures throughout the entire IoT product lifecycle. This proactive stance ensures that security considerations are not an afterthought but are woven into the fabric of IoT development.

b. Interoperability and Compatibility

Industry standards provide a common language for IoT devices. Adhering to these standards enhances interoperability, enabling devices from different manufacturers to work seamlessly together. This interoperability is crucial for the scalability and widespread adoption of IoT solutions.

c. Trust and Consumer Confidence

Compliance with industry standards builds trust among consumers, businesses, and regulatory bodies. Demonstrating adherence to recognized standards signals a commitment to security and reliability, instilling confidence in the integrity of IoT products and services.

4. Challenges in IoT Compliance

a. Diverse Ecosystem and Standards Fragmentation

The IoT landscape is characterized by diversity, with devices ranging from smart home gadgets to industrial sensors. Navigating this diversity presents challenges, as standards may vary across sectors, leading to potential fragmentation and interoperability issues.

b. Evolving Threat Landscape

The rapid evolution of the IoT threat landscape demands continuous adaptation of standards. New vulnerabilities and attack vectors require industry standards to evolve to address emerging security challenges effectively.

5. Future Directions and Adaptability

a. Regulatory Evolution

As IoT matures, regulatory bodies are expected to refine and expand compliance requirements. Industry stakeholders must remain adaptable, anticipating and aligning with evolving regulatory landscapes.

b. International Collaboration

Efforts toward international collaboration are vital to harmonizing IoT standards globally. Initiatives that promote cooperation among standardization bodies and regulatory agencies can contribute to a more cohesive and effective IoT security framework.

6. Conclusion

In conclusion, compliance with regulatory requirements and adherence to industry standards are non-negotiable imperatives in the IoT landscape. The regulatory and standards frameworks provide a roadmap for developing and deploying secure IoT solutions, ensuring data protection, privacy, and the overall integrity of connected ecosystems. As IoT continues to evolve, the commitment to compliance will be instrumental in building a resilient, trustworthy, and secure IoT future.

This exploration emphasizes the critical importance of meeting compliance requirements and following industry standards in the IoT sector, providing a foundation for secure and responsible IoT development and deployment.

Global efforts to establish a unified framework for IoT security

The proliferation of the Internet of Things (IoT) has propelled connectivity into nearly every facet of our lives, from smart homes to industrial automation. Yet, this rapid expansion has exposed significant security challenges, necessitating a collective and international response. This exploration delves into the ongoing global efforts to establish a unified framework for IoT security, highlighting the collaborative initiatives and challenges on the path to a cohesive and resilient security landscape.

1. The Need for a Unified Framework

a. Diverse Ecosystem Challenges

The diverse nature of the IoT ecosystem, spanning industries and applications, poses challenges in establishing consistent security measures. A unified framework becomes imperative to address the unique security requirements across sectors, ensuring a cohesive approach to mitigating risks.

b. Global Interconnectedness

As IoT devices transcend geographical boundaries, the impact of security vulnerabilities becomes global. A unified framework is crucial to create a baseline of security standards that can be universally applied, fostering a more secure and interconnected digital environment.

2. International Standards Organizations

a. ISO/IEC JTC 1/SC 41 for IoT and Related Technologies

The International Organization for Standardization (ISO) and the International Electrotechnical Commission (IEC) Joint Technical Committee (JTC) 1, Subcommittee (SC) 41 focuses on IoT and related technologies. It aims to develop standards to ensure the security, interoperability, and sustainability of IoT deployments on a global scale.

b. ITU-T SG20 for IoT and its applications, including smart cities and communities

The International Telecommunication Union Telecommunication Standardization Sector (ITU-T) Study Group 20 is dedicated to IoT standardization. Its focus extends to smart cities and communities, recognizing the interconnected nature of IoT in shaping the future of urban environments.

3. Regional and Cross-Industry Collaborations

a. EU Cybersecurity Act

In the European Union, the Cybersecurity Act aims to enhance the EU's cybersecurity framework. While not exclusive to IoT, it emphasizes the importance of common criteria and certification schemes, contributing to a harmonized approach to cybersecurity that can benefit IoT deployments.

b. Industrial Internet Consortium (IIC)

The IIC is a global organization that brings together industry leaders to accelerate the adoption of the Industrial Internet of Things (IIoT). While focused on industrial applications, the IIC's efforts contribute to the broader discourse on IoT security standards and practices.

4. Challenges and Considerations

a. Industry-Specific Requirements

Balancing the need for a unified framework with industry-specific requirements poses challenges. Certain sectors may require tailored security measures, and finding common ground without compromising sector-specific needs is a delicate task.

b. Evolving Threat Landscape

The dynamic nature of cyber threats requires constant adaptation. A unified framework must be flexible and responsive to emerging threats, incorporating mechanisms for regular updates and improvements to address evolving cybersecurity challenges.

5. Future Directions and Opportunities

a. Cross-Sector Collaboration

Fostering collaboration not only within the IoT sector but also across industries and sectors is crucial. Cross-sector collaboration allows for the exchange of best practices, lessons learned, and the development of comprehensive security frameworks that encompass diverse use cases.

b. Public-Private Partnerships

Engaging in public-private partnerships can enhance the effectiveness of global efforts. Collaboration between governments, regulatory bodies, and private-sector entities can contribute to the development and implementation of robust and widely accepted IoT security standards.

6. Conclusion

In conclusion, the journey towards a unified framework for IoT security is marked by global collaboration, standardization efforts, and the recognition of the interconnectedness of the digital landscape. While challenges persist, the commitment to establishing common standards is a testament to the shared responsibility of securing the IoT ecosystem. As the world becomes increasingly connected, a unified framework for IoT security is not just desirable; it is imperative for the sustainable and secure evolution of our digitally intertwined future.

6. IoT Authentication and Access Control

The significance of robust authentication mechanisms for IoT devices

The proliferation of the Internet of Things (IoT) has ushered in an era of unprecedented connectivity, seamlessly integrating devices into our daily lives and industrial processes. However, with this interconnectedness comes a critical challenge: how to secure the vast network of IoT devices against potential threats. At the forefront of this challenge lies the significance of robust authentication mechanisms. This exploration delves into the pivotal role of authentication in the IoT landscape, highlighting its importance, challenges, and the evolving landscape of access control.

1. The Foundation of IoT Security

a. Inherent Vulnerabilities of IoT Devices

IoT devices, ranging from smart thermostats to industrial sensors, often operate in environments where security considerations were not initially a priority. Their resource constraints, coupled with the sheer diversity of devices, create a fertile ground for potential vulnerabilities. Robust authentication serves as the bedrock upon which a secure IoT ecosystem can be built.

b. The Expanding Attack Surface

As the number of connected devices burgeons, so does the attack surface. Each IoT device represents a potential entry point for cyber threats. Robust authentication mechanisms are the first line of defense, ensuring that only authorized entities can access and interact with these devices.

2. The Pillars of Authentication in IoT

a. Device Authentication

Device authentication is fundamental in ensuring that only legitimate devices can connect to the IoT network. This process involves verifying the identity of devices through secure mechanisms such as digital certificates or unique identifiers. Device-level authentication establishes a foundation of trust within the IoT ecosystem.

b. User Authentication

In scenarios where user interaction with IoT devices is prevalent, user authentication becomes paramount. Whether it's a smart home application or an industrial control system, verifying the identity of users mitigates the risk of unauthorized access and safeguards sensitive data.

3. Challenges in IoT Authentication

a. Resource Constraints

Many IoT devices operate with limited computational power and memory. Implementing robust authentication while respecting these resource constraints requires innovative solutions such as lightweight cryptographic algorithms and efficient key management.

b. Heterogeneity of Devices

The diverse landscape of IoT devices, each with its own set of communication protocols and security capabilities, poses a challenge for standardizing authentication mechanisms. The industry must navigate this heterogeneity to establish universal best practices.

4. Evolving Landscape: Multi-Factor Authentication (MFA) in IoT

a. Strengthening Security with Multi-Factor Authentication

As threats evolve, the need for multi-faceted security measures becomes imperative. Multi-Factor Authentication (MFA), involving the use of multiple authentication factors such as passwords, biometrics, and one-time codes, adds an additional layer of security to IoT deployments. MFA is particularly relevant in scenarios where the compromise of a single authentication factor is deemed high risk.

b. Biometrics and Behavioral Authentication

In the pursuit of enhancing user authentication, the integration of biometrics and behavioral authentication is gaining traction. Biometric markers such as fingerprints or facial recognition, coupled with behavioral patterns like typing speed or device interaction habits, provide a more nuanced and secure authentication approach.

5. Access Control in IoT Ecosystems

a. Granular Control over Device Access

Authentication is intrinsically linked with access control. Once the identity of a device or user is established, access control mechanisms define the level of permissions granted. Granular control ensures that each entity within the IoT ecosystem has access only to the resources and functionalities necessary for its intended purpose.

b. Role-Based Access Control (RBAC)

Implementing Role-Based Access Control assigns specific roles and associated permissions to users or devices based on their functions within the IoT ecosystem. This approach streamlines access management, reducing the risk of unauthorized actions.

6. The Human Element: Educating Users on IoT Security

a. Importance of User Awareness

In IoT scenarios involving user interaction, the human element becomes a crucial factor. Educating users about the significance of strong authentication practices, the potential risks of weak passwords, and the importance of promptly updating credentials enhances the overall security posture of IoT deployments.

b. Balancing Convenience and Security

Striking a balance between security and user convenience is an ongoing challenge. Implementing user-friendly authentication processes, such as biometric recognition or seamless device pairing, encourages adherence to security measures without compromising usability.

7. Future Directions: Zero Trust Security Model in IoT

a. Zero Trust Paradigm

The Zero Trust security model, which operates under the assumption that no entity—whether inside or outside the network—should be trusted by default, holds promise for IoT security. Implementing Zero Trust principles in IoT architectures involves continuous verification of device and user identities, bolstering overall security resilience.

b. Integration of Artificial Intelligence (AI)

The integration of artificial intelligence (AI) in authentication processes introduces adaptive and context-aware security measures. AI-driven authentication continuously analyzes user and device behavior, adapting security protocols in real-time to counter emerging threats.

8. Conclusion: Safeguarding the IoT Nexus

In conclusion, robust authentication mechanisms form the bedrock of IoT security. As the IoT landscape continues to expand and diversify, the industry must evolve authentication practices to meet the challenges of resource constraints, device heterogeneity, and evolving threats. The integration of multi-factor authentication, biometrics, and adaptive access control, coupled with user education, is essential for creating a secure and resilient IoT ecosystem. Looking ahead, the adoption of emerging paradigms like the Zero Trust model and the infusion of AI into authentication processes will further fortify the defense against cyber threats, safeguarding the interconnected web of IoT devices.

The role of access control in limiting unauthorized access to IoT systems

The interconnected tapestry of the Internet of Things (IoT) introduces a myriad of devices into our homes, industries, and daily lives. Yet, with this seamless connectivity comes the pressing need to fortify these digital gateways against unauthorized access. Access control emerges as the sentinel at the forefront, tasked with delineating who gains entry and under what circumstances. This exploration unravels the pivotal role of access control in limiting unauthorized access to IoT systems, delving into its significance, mechanisms, challenges, and the evolving landscape of digital guardianship.

1. Fortifying the Digital Perimeter

a. The Expanding IoT Frontier

As the number of IoT devices burgeons, each device becomes a potential entry point for malicious actors. Access control serves as the digital gatekeeper, determining who can interact with these devices, access sensitive data, or issue commands. Its role is fundamental in safeguarding the integrity of the IoT ecosystem.

b. Unauthorized Access: A Potent Threat

Unauthorized access to IoT systems can have far-reaching consequences. From privacy breaches in smart homes to the compromise of critical industrial processes, the implications underscore the urgency of robust access control mechanisms.

2. The Mechanisms of Access Control in IoT

a. Authentication as the Vanguard

Authentication is the first line of defense in access control. Verifying the identity of users and devices ensures that only authorized entities gain entry. From traditional username-password combinations to advanced methods like biometric recognition, authentication lays the groundwork for secure access.

b. Authorization: Defining Permissions

Once authenticated, entities must undergo authorization. Authorization delineates the level of permissions granted to a user or device. Role-Based Access Control (RBAC) and Attribute-Based Access Control (ABAC) are common paradigms, allowing for granular control over the actions each entity can perform within the IoT system.

3. Challenges in Implementing Access Control for IoT

a. Device Heterogeneity

The diverse array of IoT devices, each with its own set of capabilities and communication protocols, poses a challenge for uniform access control. Implementing standardized mechanisms across this heterogeneity demands innovative solutions.

b. Resource Constraints

Many IoT devices operate with limited resources, making resource-efficient access control paramount. Lightweight cryptographic algorithms and efficient authorization processes are essential to ensure that access control doesn't strain device capabilities.

4. Evolving Landscape: Adaptive Access Control

a. Dynamic Security Measures

As cyber threats evolve, access control mechanisms must adapt. Adaptive Access Control involves continuous assessment of user and device behavior. Deviations from established patterns trigger alerts or adjustments in access permissions, enhancing the system's resilience against emerging threats.

b. Context-Aware Access Control

Context-aware access control takes into account the environmental context in which access requests occur. Factors such as location, time of day, and the type of device used contribute to the decision-making process, adding an extra layer of intelligence to access control.

5. Ensuring Privacy and Data Protection

a. Privacy-Preserving Access Control

Privacy is a paramount concern in IoT systems, particularly in scenarios involving personal data. Privacy-preserving access control mechanisms, such as differential privacy and secure multiparty computation, ensure that access control doesn't compromise individual privacy.

b. Data Encryption and Transit Security

Securing data in transit is integral to access control. Encryption protocols safeguard communication channels between devices and the broader IoT network, preventing unauthorized interception of sensitive information.

6. The Human Element: User-Centric Access Control

a. Empowering Users

In scenarios where human interaction with IoT systems is prevalent, user-centric access control becomes pivotal. Empowering users with control over their device permissions and fostering awareness about access settings enhances security while respecting user autonomy.

b. Balancing Usability and Security

Striking a balance between user-friendly interfaces and robust security measures is crucial. Access control mechanisms should be designed to minimize friction for legitimate users while deterring unauthorized access.

7. Future Directions: Zero Trust Security Model in IoT Access Control

a. Rethinking Trust Assumptions

The Zero Trust security model challenges the traditional notion of trust, assuming that no entity—whether inside or outside the network—should be trusted by default. Implementing Zero Trust principles in access control involves continuous verification and validation of user and device identities.

b. Integration of Artificial Intelligence (AI)

The infusion of artificial intelligence (AI) into access control processes introduces adaptive and context-aware security measures. AI-driven access control continuously analyzes user and device behavior, adapting access permissions in real-time to counter emerging threats.

8. Conclusion: Custodians of Connectivity

In conclusion, access control stands as the custodian of connectivity in the IoT landscape. Its role in limiting unauthorized access is foundational to the security and integrity of IoT systems. As the digital frontier expands, access control mechanisms must evolve, embracing adaptability, intelligence, and user-centricity. The integration of emerging paradigms like the Zero Trust model and AI-driven access control heralds a future where unauthorized access is not just deterred but actively thwarted, ensuring the custodianship of IoT connectivity remains steadfast.

The challenges of managing credentials for a multitude of interconnected devices

In the fields of the Internet of Things (IoT), where devices seamlessly communicate to orchestrate the intricacies of modern life, lies a formidable challenge - managing credentials for a multitude of interconnected devices. As the number of IoT devices burgeons, each with its own identity and access requirements, the task of credential management becomes a complex puzzle. This exploration unravels the challenges inherent in managing credentials for a vast array of interconnected devices, delving into the complexities, security implications, and strategies to navigate the credential maze.

1. The Scale of Credential Management in IoT

a. The Proliferation of Devices

The proliferation of IoT devices in homes, industries, and cities is staggering. From smart thermostats and wearables to industrial sensors and autonomous vehicles, each device requires a unique identity, and, consequently, a set of credentials for secure authentication and access.

b. Credential Diversity

IoT devices vary widely in their capabilities and communication protocols. Managing credentials involves dealing with diverse authentication methods, encryption standards, and key management practices, adding layers of complexity to the credential management landscape.

2. Security Implications of Credential Management in IoT

a. Authentication Risks

As the number of devices grows, so does the risk of unauthorized access. Weak or compromised credentials pose a significant threat, potentially providing malicious actors with entry points to exploit vulnerabilities in the IoT ecosystem.

b. Credential Theft and Tampering

Theft or tampering of credentials is a critical concern. Unauthorized access to device credentials can lead to data breaches, privacy violations, and, in certain scenarios, physical harm if the compromised device controls critical infrastructure.

3. Challenges in Credential Lifecycle Management

a. Provisioning and Onboarding

The process of provisioning and onboarding IoT devices involves assigning initial credentials. Managing this step efficiently while ensuring secure distribution of credentials to devices poses a logistical challenge, especially in scenarios with a large number of devices.

b. Key Rotation and Updates

Ensuring the security of IoT systems requires regular key rotation and updates. Coordinating the timely rotation of cryptographic keys without disrupting device functionality is a complex task, particularly in environments with stringent uptime requirements.

4. Resource Constraints in IoT Devices

a. Limited Computational Power and Memory

Many IoT devices operate with limited computational power and memory. Implementing robust cryptographic algorithms and secure key storage mechanisms within these constraints requires careful optimization and innovation in credential management practices.

b. Energy Efficiency Considerations

Energy-efficient operation is paramount for battery-powered IoT devices. Credential management processes should minimize energy consumption during authentication and encryption processes to extend the operational life of these devices.

5. Interoperability Challenges

a. Diverse Communication Protocols

The diversity of communication protocols among IoT devices introduces interoperability challenges in credential management. Standardizing authentication methods across devices with varying communication standards requires industry-wide collaboration and standardization efforts.

b. Vendor-Specific Implementations

Vendor-specific implementations of credential management can lead to inconsistencies in security practices. Encouraging adherence to industry standards and promoting interoperability can mitigate challenges arising from diverse vendor approaches.

6. Credential Revocation and Decommissioning

a. Responding to Compromised Credentials

In the event of a security incident or the detection of compromised credentials, swift action is required to revoke and replace affected credentials. Managing the timely revocation and replacement of credentials on a large scale is a challenge that necessitates efficient response mechanisms.

b. Decommissioning End-of-Life Devices

As devices reach the end of their operational life, proper credential decommissioning is crucial. Ensuring that decommissioned devices no longer possess valid credentials mitigates the risk of unauthorized access or potential reuse of credentials in nefarious activities.

7. Human Element: User Interaction and Authentication

a. User-Friendly Authentication Processes

In scenarios where user interaction with IoT devices is prevalent, designing user-friendly authentication processes is essential. Simplifying credential management for end-users without compromising security is a delicate balancing act.

b. Education and Awareness

Educating users about the importance of strong credentials, password hygiene, and the potential risks associated with weak or shared credentials contributes to a more secure IoT ecosystem. Raising awareness fosters a culture of cybersecurity among end-users.

8. Future Strategies and Innovations in Credential Management

a. Blockchain for Decentralized Identity

Blockchain technology holds promise for decentralized identity management. Implementing blockchain-based solutions can enhance the security and integrity of credential management by providing a tamper-resistant ledger of device identities and credentials.

b. Zero Trust Security Model Integration

Integrating the Zero Trust security model involves continuous verification of device identities and permissions. This model challenges traditional assumptions about trust, enhancing security by adopting a "never trust, always verify" approach.

9. Conclusion: Orchestrating Security in the IoT Symphony

In conclusion, managing credentials for a multitude of interconnected devices in the IoT landscape is a multifaceted challenge. The scale, security implications, and diverse nature of IoT devices demand innovative solutions and collaborative efforts. Navigating the credential maze requires a strategic approach that encompasses secure provisioning, efficient key management, and continuous adaptation to evolving security threats. As the IoT ecosystem evolves, the industry must remain vigilant, embracing emerging technologies and best practices to orchestrate a secure symphony of interconnected devices.

7. IoT Firmware Security

Security considerations of IoT device firmware

As the bridge between hardware and software, IoT device firmware plays a pivotal role in ensuring seamless operations. This exploration delves into the critical security considerations surrounding IoT device firmware, unraveling the complexities, vulnerabilities, and strategies to fortify the digital sentinels that underpin the IoT ecosystem.

The Heart of IoT: Understanding Firmware

Firmware serves as the embedded software that orchestrates the behavior of IoT devices. It resides on the device's non-volatile memory, acting as the intermediary between the hardware components and the software applications that enable device functionality. Many IoT devices operate within the constraints of embedded systems with limited computational power and memory. Firmware must be optimized for efficiency, making security considerations a delicate balance between robust protection and resource efficiency.

Vulnerabilities in IoT Firmware

Vulnerabilities often stem from insecure coding practices during firmware development. Flaws such as buffer overflows, improper input validation, and insecure data storage can expose vulnerabilities that adversaries may exploit. The absence of robust encryption mechanisms can lead to unauthorized access, and encrypting data at rest and in transit within the firmware is crucial for preventing data breaches.

Over-the-Air (OTA) Updates: A Double-Edged Sword

OTA updates are a common mechanism for patching vulnerabilities, introducing new features, and enhancing the overall security of IoT devices. However, managing the security of these updates is a critical concern. Insecure OTA processes can become entry points for attackers. Lack of encryption, weak authentication, or compromised update servers can be exploited to deliver malicious firmware, compromising the entire device.

Secure Boot Processes: Fortifying Device Integrity

Secure boot processes ensure that only authenticated and unaltered firmware is loaded during device startup. This foundational security measure safeguards against firmware tampering and unauthorized code execution. Establishing a chain of trust, where each stage in the boot process verifies the integrity of the subsequent stage, enhances the security of the boot process. Any compromise in this chain triggers security alerts and prevents the device from loading compromised firmware.

IoT Firmware Authentication and Authorization

Firmware authentication ensures that only legitimate and authorized firmware updates are accepted. Strong cryptographic verification of the firmware's digital signature helps prevent the installation of malicious or unauthorized code. Implementing role-based authorization within firmware determines the level of access and functionality each component or module has. This granular control mitigates the impact of potential breaches, restricting unauthorized actions.

Encryption and Data Protection

Encrypting sensitive information within the firmware is paramount. Passwords, cryptographic keys, and other confidential data must be stored and transmitted securely to prevent unauthorized access and data breaches. Leveraging hardware-based encryption mechanisms enhances security by offloading encryption processes to dedicated hardware components. This not only improves performance but also adds an additional layer of protection against software-based attacks.

Threat Modeling in Firmware Development

Threat modeling during the firmware development phase involves systematically identifying potential security threats and vulnerabilities. This proactive approach enables developers to implement security measures tailored to the specific risks associated with the device and its environment. Conducting regular security assessments, including penetration testing and code reviews, ensures that firmware remains resilient to evolving threats. Continuous monitoring and updates based on threat intelligence contribute to a dynamic defense against emerging risks.

Conclusion: Safeguarding the Digital Core

In conclusion, the security considerations of IoT device firmware are paramount in fortifying the digital core of the IoT ecosystem. From the secure boot processes that establish device integrity to the complexities of managing over-the-air updates, every facet of firmware development requires meticulous attention to security. As the IoT landscape evolves, so do the threats, emphasizing the need for ongoing innovation and vigilance in the realm of firmware security. By embracing robust encryption, authentication, and authorization practices, the guardians of the code ensure that IoT devices stand resilient against the ever-present challenges of the digital frontier.

The importance of secure boot processes and firmware updates

The bedrock of security lies in the diligent implementation of two key processes: secure boot and firmware updates. These mechanisms serve as the vanguards, fortifying IoT devices against unauthorized access, tampering, and vulnerabilities. This exploration delves into the pivotal role of secure boot processes and firmware updates in ensuring the robust security posture of IoT devices, unraveling their importance, challenges, and the evolving landscape of digital defense.

The Significance of Secure Boot Processes in IoT

In the realm of IoT, where devices operate in diverse and often unpredictable environments, the secure boot process stands as the first line of defense. This process ensures that only authenticated and unaltered firmware is loaded during the device's startup sequence. Its importance can be dissected into several critical facets:

• Preventing Unauthorized Code Execution: Secure boot establishes a chain of trust, requiring each stage in the boot process to verify the integrity of the subsequent stage. This prevents unauthorized code execution and safeguards the device against malicious firmware.

• Protecting Against Firmware Tampering: By verifying the digital signatures of firmware components, secure boot processes mitigate the risk of firmware tampering. Any attempt to introduce unauthorized changes triggers security alerts, preserving the integrity of the device's firmware.

• Defending Against Supply Chain Attacks: Secure boot processes play a pivotal role in mitigating supply chain attacks. By ensuring that only firmware from trusted sources is executed, these processes guard against compromised firmware infiltrating the device during manufacturing or distribution.

Challenges in Implementing Secure Boot Processes for IoT Devices

While the benefits of secure boot processes are evident, their implementation in the diverse landscape of IoT devices is not without challenges:

• Resource Constraints: Many IoT devices operate with limited computational power and memory. Implementing robust secure boot processes that are both effective and resource-efficient poses a significant challenge.

• Diverse Hardware Platforms: The IoT ecosystem encompasses a wide array of hardware platforms, each with its own specifications. Adapting secure boot processes to cater to this diversity requires standardized approaches and collaboration within the industry.

• Balancing Security and Usability: Striking a balance between robust security measures and user-friendly experiences is crucial. Secure boot processes should be designed to minimize disruption for legitimate users while thwarting malicious attempts.

The Dynamic Role of Firmware Updates in IoT Security

Firmware updates serve as the lifeline for IoT devices, enabling manufacturers to rectify vulnerabilities, introduce new features, and enhance overall security. The importance of firmware updates can be elucidated through various dimensions:

• Patch Management and Vulnerability Mitigation: In the ever-evolving threat landscape, vulnerabilities may emerge post-deployment. Firmware updates provide a mechanism to swiftly address these vulnerabilities, ensuring that devices remain resilient to emerging threats.

- Introducing Security Enhancements: As security standards evolve, firmware updates allow manufacturers to implement advanced security measures. This might include improved encryption algorithms, enhanced authentication mechanisms, or the integration of security patches from third-party libraries.

- Addressing Regulatory Compliance: With the emergence of stringent cybersecurity regulations, firmware updates play a crucial role in ensuring compliance. Manufacturers can use updates to align their devices with evolving regulatory requirements, enhancing the overall security posture.

Challenges in Implementing Firmware Updates for IoT Devices

Despite their pivotal role, firmware updates pose challenges in their implementation for IoT devices:

- Over-the-Air (OTA) Security: The delivery of firmware updates over the air introduces security concerns. Ensuring the integrity and authenticity of updates during transmission is critical to prevent malicious actors from intercepting or manipulating the update process.

- Device Compatibility: The diverse range of IoT devices, each with its unique specifications, poses challenges in ensuring that firmware updates are compatible across various platforms. Manufacturers must develop standardized approaches to address compatibility issues.

- User Awareness and Adoption: Encouraging users to promptly apply firmware updates is a significant challenge. Awareness campaigns, user-friendly update mechanisms, and transparent communication about the importance of updates play a crucial role in overcoming this challenge.

The Convergence: Enhancing Security through Synergy

The synergy between secure boot processes and firmware updates forms the cornerstone of a resilient IoT security strategy:

- Continuous Defense Posture: Secure boot processes establish a secure foundation, and firmware updates contribute to the ongoing defense posture. Together, they create a dynamic security environment capable of adapting to emerging threats.

- Adaptive Response to Threats: The combination of secure boot and firmware updates allows devices to adapt to evolving threats. Secure boot provides immediate protection during startup, while firmware updates address vulnerabilities and enhance security over time.

- Regulatory Compliance: The convergence of secure boot processes and firmware updates assists manufacturers in meeting regulatory requirements. By implementing robust security measures from the device's inception and continuously addressing vulnerabilities, compliance becomes an integral part of the device lifecycle.

Conclusion: Safeguarding the IoT Frontier

In conclusion, the importance of secure boot processes and firmware updates in the realm of IoT cannot be overstated. They are not isolated measures but integral components of a holistic security strategy. Secure boot processes establish the device's initial defense, while firmware updates ensure its resilience in the face of an ever-shifting threat landscape. As the IoT ecosystem continues to burgeon, manufacturers, developers, and users must recognize the symbiotic relationship between these processes and work collaboratively to fortify the digital frontier against emerging threats.

Exploring techniques for ensuring the integrity and authenticity of IoT device firmware

In the dynamic landscape of the Internet of Things (IoT), where devices interconnect to orchestrate the fabric of modern life, ensuring the integrity and authenticity of device firmware is paramount. Trust in the digital realm hinges on the ability to guarantee that the firmware running on IoT devices is both unaltered and originates from a legitimate source. This exploration delves into the intricate techniques that serve as the guardians of trust, safeguarding the very core of IoT ecosystems against malicious alterations, unauthorized access, and potential vulnerabilities.

1. Digital Signatures: Cryptographic Imprints of Authenticity
At the forefront of techniques ensuring firmware integrity and authenticity are digital signatures. Cryptographic in nature, digital signatures provide a tamper-evident seal on firmware, confirming that it has not been altered since the signature was applied. This involves using asymmetric key pairs, where the private key signs the firmware during development, and the public key verifies the signature during deployment. Any tampering or unauthorized modification would break the digital signature, alerting the system to potential compromise.

2. Hash Functions: Verifying Data Integrity
Hash functions play a pivotal role in verifying the integrity of IoT device firmware. By generating a fixed-size hash value based on the firmware's content, any change, no matter how minute, results in a vastly different hash. During the verification process, the hash of the received firmware is compared to the precomputed hash stored securely on the device. A mismatch signals potential tampering, prompting the system to reject the compromised firmware.

3. Secure Boot Processes: Establishing a Chain of Trust
Secure boot processes serve as the bedrock for establishing a chain of trust during the startup of an IoT device. These processes involve verifying the integrity and authenticity of each component in the boot sequence, ensuring that only trusted firmware is executed. By employing digital signatures and cryptographic verification, secure boot processes thwart unauthorized attempts to load malicious or altered firmware, maintaining the device's trustworthiness from the moment it powers on.

4. Code Signing: An Additional Layer of Verification
Code signing complements digital signatures by associating a unique signature with each executable piece of code within the firmware. This granular approach allows for targeted verification, enabling the system to assess the authenticity and integrity of specific modules or updates rather than the entire firmware. Code signing is particularly valuable in scenarios where partial updates or modular additions to the firmware are common.

5. Trusted Platform Modules (TPMs): Hardware-Backed Assurance
Trusted Platform Modules, embedded hardware components dedicated to security functions, provide an

additional layer of assurance for firmware integrity. TPMs store cryptographic keys used in the verification process in a secure hardware enclave, making it significantly harder for attackers to manipulate or compromise these keys. Leveraging TPMs strengthens the overall security posture of the device, enhancing the trustworthiness of the firmware.

6. Version Control and Repository Management

Beyond cryptographic measures, effective version control and repository management are crucial for maintaining the integrity of IoT device firmware. By utilizing version control systems, developers can track changes, revert to known good states, and ensure that only authorized modifications are applied. Coupled with secure repositories, this ensures that only authenticated and approved firmware versions are accessible, reducing the risk of inadvertent or malicious alterations.

7. Secure Communication Channels: Safeguarding the Update Process

Ensuring the integrity and authenticity of firmware updates requires secure communication channels. Employing encryption and secure protocols during the update process prevents man-in-the-middle attacks and tampering during transmission. By verifying the source and integrity of the firmware update before installation, IoT devices can confidently apply updates without the risk of accepting compromised code.

8. Continuous Monitoring and Anomaly Detection

A proactive approach involves continuous monitoring of the IoT device's behavior and firmware state. Anomaly detection mechanisms can flag unexpected changes or deviations from the established baseline, triggering alerts and responses to potential security incidents. Continuous monitoring adds a dynamic layer of defense, allowing for real-time responses to emerging threats.

Conclusion: Upholding the Pillars of Trust

In conclusion, the techniques ensuring the integrity and authenticity of IoT device firmware form the pillars of trust that uphold the foundation of secure IoT ecosystems. Through cryptographic measures, hardware-backed assurances, and diligent management practices, these techniques collectively contribute to fortifying devices against malicious alterations and unauthorized access. As the IoT landscape evolves, the guardians of trust must remain vigilant, adapting and innovating to stay ahead of emerging threats and vulnerabilities.

8. IoT Ethical Hacking

The concept of ethical hacking for IoT security

1. Unveiling Ethical Hacking in the IoT Landscape: A Holistic Exploration

a. Defining Ethical Hacking: Decoding the Sentinel of Security

At the core of cybersecurity within the Internet of Things (IoT) lies the strategic practice of ethical hacking. Often interchangeably referred to as penetration testing or white-hat hacking, ethical hacking involves the purposeful and authorized endeavor to circumvent security measures. The primary objective is to meticulously identify vulnerabilities within a system, an undertaking of paramount importance in the dynamic and interconnected realm of IoT.

In the context of the IoT landscape, ethical hackers bring their expertise to bear on assessing the security posture of a myriad of interconnected devices, networks, and ecosystems. This nuanced approach recognizes the unique challenges posed by the diverse range of IoT devices, from smart home appliances to industrial sensors. The scope of ethical hacking extends beyond traditional cybersecurity paradigms, encompassing the intricacies of IoT protocols, communication frameworks, and the complex relationships between devices.

b. The Ethical Hacker's Code: Guardians of Digital Morality

Ethical hackers are not mere cyber warriors; they are guardians of digital morality operating within a structured and principled framework. Adhering to a stringent code of conduct, these professionals ensure that every action is not only legal but also authorized, carrying the explicit purpose of enhancing security. The ethical hacker's mission is to mirror the tactics employed by malicious hackers with an altruistic twist – to identify weaknesses before malevolent actors can exploit them for nefarious purposes.

This code of ethics encompasses a commitment to transparency, integrity, and a steadfast focus on improvement. Ethical hackers operate with a sense of responsibility, recognizing the impact their findings can have on the overall security of IoT ecosystems. Their actions are not driven by malintent but rather by an unwavering dedication to fortifying the digital landscape against potential threats.

Delving Deeper into Ethical Hacking Methodologies for IoT Security

As we unravel the layers of ethical hacking within the IoT landscape, it becomes imperative to explore the intricate methodologies employed by these guardians of digital security. Ethical hacking is not a monolithic process; rather, it involves a strategic and multifaceted approach tailored to the unique challenges posed by IoT devices and ecosystems. The next sections will delve into the methodologies, challenges, and future prospects of ethical hacking within the expansive domain of the Internet of Things.

2. The Stakes in IoT Security: Navigating the Expanding Frontier

a. The Growing Attack Surface: Unveiling the Complexity

In the ever-evolving landscape of the Internet of Things (IoT), the concept of the attack surface takes on profound significance. As IoT devices permeate various facets of our daily lives, from the convenience of smart homes to the intricacies of critical industrial infrastructure, the attack surface expands exponentially. This expansion is not merely linear but represents a dynamic and multifaceted web of potential vulnerabilities. Ethical hackers, donned as digital sentinels, embark on a mission to uncover and fortify this complex and sprawling attack surface.

The diversity of IoT devices adds an additional layer of intricacy to this expanding landscape. From connected thermostats and smart refrigerators to industrial sensors orchestrating complex manufacturing processes, the sheer variety of devices introduces a multitude of entry points for potential threats. Each device, operating within its unique ecosystem and communication protocols, becomes a node in the vast tapestry of the IoT attack surface. Ethical hackers, armed with specialized skills and a deep understanding of IoT intricacies, are tasked with navigating this intricate web to identify vulnerabilities before malicious actors can exploit them.

As the attack surface grows, ethical hackers recognize the need for a nuanced and adaptive approach. Their methodology extends beyond conventional cybersecurity practices, encompassing the specific challenges posed by the diversity of IoT devices, the intricate interplay of communication protocols, and the potential cascading effects of vulnerabilities within interconnected ecosystems.

b. Consequences of IoT Security Breaches: Navigating the Minefield

The consequences of security breaches in the IoT space transcend the realm of inconvenience, venturing into the territory of severe repercussions. In this minefield of potential threats, ethical hacking emerges as a preemptive strike against the impending dangers, providing organizations with the means to bolster their defenses and shield against real-world attacks.

Unauthorized Access to Sensitive Data:

One of the immediate and pervasive consequences of an IoT security breach is the risk of unauthorized access to sensitive data. In the interconnected world of IoT, devices often handle a trove of personal and confidential information. From smart home cameras capturing intimate moments to industrial sensors collecting proprietary data, the ramifications of unauthorized access can be profound. Ethical hackers, through meticulous assessments, strive to fortify the defenses guarding this sensitive data, ensuring that it remains beyond the reach of malicious entities.

Manipulation of Critical Infrastructure:

The integration of IoT devices into critical infrastructure, such as energy grids, transportation systems, and healthcare facilities, underscores the potential impact of security breaches. Malevolent actors, if successful in exploiting vulnerabilities, can manipulate critical systems with far-reaching consequences. The manipulation of energy grids could lead to power outages, interference with transportation systems could pose safety hazards, and compromise of healthcare IoT devices could jeopardize patient well-being. Ethical hacking becomes a strategic imperative to safeguard these critical infrastructures from the debilitating effects of manipulation.

Erosion of User Privacy and Trust:

As IoT devices become integral to our daily lives, user privacy assumes paramount importance. Security breaches that compromise user data erode the trust that individuals place in these interconnected systems. The consequences extend beyond immediate financial or operational impacts,

105

encompassing the long-term erosion of user confidence in the reliability and security of IoT devices. Ethical hackers, by uncovering and addressing vulnerabilities, play a pivotal role in preserving user privacy and bolstering the trust essential for the continued adoption of IoT technologies.

Financial and Reputational Fallout:

The fallout from IoT security breaches is not confined to the digital realm but extends into the financial and reputational domains. Organizations that fall victim to security breaches may incur significant financial losses, ranging from remediation costs to legal ramifications. Moreover, the reputational damage resulting from a compromised security posture can have enduring consequences, impacting customer trust, investor confidence, and overall brand integrity. Ethical hacking serves as a proactive measure to mitigate these potential risks, allowing organizations to fortify their defenses against the financial and reputational fallout of security breaches.

Ethical Hacking: A Proactive Defense Against Impending Threats

In the face of the expanding attack surface and the potential consequences of security breaches in the IoT space, ethical hacking emerges as a proactive and strategic defense mechanism. Ethical hackers, armed with a comprehensive understanding of IoT intricacies, undertake a multifaceted approach to identify, assess, and fortify vulnerabilities before they can be exploited by malicious entities.

Navigating Complexity through Specialized Expertise:

The diversity of IoT devices, each operating within its unique ecosystem and communication protocols, demands specialized expertise. Ethical hackers bring a nuanced understanding of IoT intricacies, enabling them to navigate the complexities of the expanding attack surface. From connected homes to industrial IoT deployments, their expertise spans the breadth of the IoT landscape.

Strategic Assessment and Remediation:

Ethical hackers conduct strategic assessments that go beyond conventional cybersecurity practices. Their methodologies encompass the specific challenges posed by IoT devices, including the identification of potential entry points, communication vulnerabilities, and cascading effects within interconnected ecosystems. Through this strategic lens, ethical hackers provide organizations with actionable insights and targeted remediation strategies to fortify their defenses.

Preserving User Privacy and Trust:

By proactively identifying and addressing vulnerabilities, ethical hackers contribute to the preservation of user privacy and trust. Their efforts ensure that sensitive data remains secure, mitigating the risk of unauthorized access and erosion of user confidence in IoT technologies. This proactive stance is instrumental in fostering a secure and trustworthy environment for users interacting with interconnected devices.

Mitigating Financial and Reputational Risks:

Ethical hacking serves as a proactive measure to mitigate the financial and reputational risks associated with IoT security breaches. By uncovering vulnerabilities before they can be exploited, ethical hackers empower organizations to implement robust security measures, reducing the likelihood of financial losses and safeguarding their reputation in the digital landscape.

Conclusion: Ethical Hacking as the Vanguard of IoT Security

In the intricate dance between the expanding attack surface and the potential consequences of security breaches in the IoT space, ethical hacking emerges as the vanguard of defense. The dynamic landscape of IoT demands a proactive and specialized approach, one that ethical hackers embody with unwavering commitment. Their role extends beyond mere cybersecurity; it encompasses the preservation of user trust, the fortification of critical infrastructure, and the strategic defense against the multifaceted challenges posed by the IoT landscape.

3. The Methodologies of Ethical Hacking in IoT: A Tactical Unveiling

a. Reconnaissance and Information Gathering: Navigating the IoT Landscape

In the intricate dance of ethical hacking within the Internet of Things (IoT) landscape, the initial choreography involves reconnaissance and information gathering. Ethical hackers, akin to digital scouts, embark on a meticulous journey to comprehend the vast and varied IoT ecosystem's landscape. This intricate process is the critical overture, involving the identification of devices, exploration of communication protocols, and the discernment of potential entry points.

The IoT space, characterized by a multitude of devices communicating through diverse networks, necessitates a sophisticated approach to reconnaissance. Ethical hackers deploy their expertise to decipher this complex tapestry, understanding the nuances of smart homes, industrial IoT deployments, and everything in between. Identifying devices and discerning the intricacies of communication protocols become the linchpin of this initial phase, providing a foundational understanding upon which the subsequent hacking symphony unfolds.

b. Vulnerability Assessment: Unveiling Weaknesses in the IoT Fabric

Armed with a comprehensive understanding of the IoT environment, ethical hackers transition seamlessly into the next movement: vulnerability assessment. This phase is akin to pulling at the threads of the IoT fabric to reveal hidden weaknesses, misconfigurations, and potential entry points that malicious actors might exploit.

The intricacies of IoT devices, each with its unique set of protocols and functionalities, demand a tailored approach to vulnerability assessment. Ethical hackers apply their skills to unveil weaknesses that might escape conventional cybersecurity measures. Whether it be a misconfigured sensor in an industrial setting or a vulnerability in a smart home device's firmware, the assessment is meticulous and specific to the idiosyncrasies of IoT networks and protocols.

c. Exploitation and Simulation of Attacks: Orchestrating the Ethical Offensive

As the ethical hacking symphony progresses, the crescendo arrives with the exploitation and simulation of attacks. Ethical hackers, now akin to conductors orchestrating a controlled offensive, simulate real-world attacks to exploit the vulnerabilities identified in the previous movements. This involves attempts at unauthorized access, manipulation of data, and compromise of IoT device functionalities.

In the IoT space, where the consequences of security breaches can be far-reaching, the simulated attacks aim to mirror the tactics that malicious actors might employ. The goal is not only to identify weaknesses but to understand the potential impact of these vulnerabilities on the overall functionality and security of IoT ecosystems. Ethical hackers, with a strategic mindset, navigate the labyrinth of interconnected devices to recommend countermeasures that fortify against real-world threats.

d. Post-Exploitation Analysis: Deciphering the Aftermath

The denouement of the ethical hacking symphony involves post-exploitation analysis, a phase where ethical hackers meticulously decipher the aftermath of simulated attacks. This critical analysis serves as the epilogue, providing insights into the potential impact of a security breach and laying the groundwork for comprehensive remediation strategies.

After simulating attacks, ethical hackers scrutinize the data, patterns, and consequences of their actions. This detailed analysis is not only instrumental in understanding how a malicious actor might exploit vulnerabilities but also in devising effective countermeasures. Recommendations for remediation strategies, tailored to the intricacies of the IoT environment, are crafted based on this insightful post-exploitation analysis.

Ethical Hacking Methodologies: A Harmonious Defense Against IoT Threats

The methodologies of ethical hacking in the IoT space form a harmonious defense against the ever-evolving threats that permeate the digital landscape. From the nuanced reconnaissance phase, navigating the complexities of diverse IoT ecosystems, to the post-exploitation analysis that informs comprehensive remediation, ethical hackers employ a tactical symphony to fortify against potential threats.

Navigating Complexity with Precision:

The IoT ecosystem, with its diverse devices and communication protocols, demands precision in every note played by ethical hackers. Navigating this complexity requires a nuanced understanding of smart homes, industrial IoT, healthcare devices, and more. Ethical hackers act as virtuosos, ensuring that every movement in the symphony is tailored to the intricacies of the IoT landscape.

Tailored Vulnerability Assessment:

Vulnerability assessment in the IoT space is not a one-size-fits-all endeavor. Ethical hackers bring a tailored approach, uncovering weaknesses that may elude conventional cybersecurity measures. The assessment is a diagnostic tool, revealing vulnerabilities specific to IoT devices, networks, and protocols.

Orchestrating Controlled Offensives:

Simulating real-world attacks is the ethical hacker's forte. Like conductors leading an orchestra, ethical hackers orchestrate controlled offensives to exploit identified vulnerabilities. This strategic approach provides organizations with a realistic understanding of potential threats, allowing them to fortify their defenses against real-world scenarios.

Deciphering the Aftermath for Strategic Insights:

Post-exploitation analysis is not merely a conclusion but a portal to strategic insights. Ethical hackers delve into the aftermath of simulated attacks, deciphering data, patterns, and consequences. The insights gained during this phase inform comprehensive remediation strategies, ensuring that vulnerabilities are not only identified but effectively addressed.

Conclusion: Ethical Hacking as a Strategic Sonata

In the realm of IoT security, ethical hacking stands as a strategic sonata, a harmonious composition of precision, tailored methodologies, and strategic insights. Ethical hackers, through their meticulous approach, not only identify vulnerabilities but orchestrate a defense symphony that fortifies against the dynamic and ever-evolving threats within the IoT landscape.

4. The Collaborative Approach to Ethical Hacking in IoT: Fostering Security from Inception

a. Partnerships with Manufacturers and Developers: Building Security into the DNA

In the intricate dance of securing the Internet of Things (IoT), ethical hackers take center stage alongside manufacturers and developers, forging partnerships that transcend traditional cybersecurity paradigms. This collaborative approach is not a mere subplot; it's an essential act that unfolds during the design and development phases of IoT devices. Ethical hackers, akin to trusted advisors, ensure that security is not an afterthought but an integral part of the device's architecture from the very outset.

The collaboration begins in the conceptualization phase, where ethical hackers provide insights into potential vulnerabilities and security considerations. This proactive engagement ensures that security measures are ingrained in the device's DNA, mitigating vulnerabilities before devices even reach the market. Whether it's a smart home device or an industrial sensor, the collaborative efforts of ethical hackers with manufacturers and developers lay the foundation for a robust and secure IoT landscape.

b. Continuous Testing and Assessment: The Ongoing Symphony of Security

Ethical hacking is not a one-off performance but an ongoing symphony, harmonizing with the dynamic nature of the IoT landscape. In this movement, continuous testing and assessment take center stage, allowing organizations to stay ahead of emerging threats and evolving attack vectors. This strategic approach recognizes that the digital landscape is not static; it's a dynamic ecosystem where threats mutate, and vulnerabilities evolve.

Periodic penetration testing becomes a cornerstone of this continuous testing approach. Ethical hackers, acting as vigilant guardians, simulate real-world attacks at regular intervals, uncovering vulnerabilities that may emerge over time. This ongoing process ensures that organizations are not merely reactive but proactive in fortifying their defenses against the ever-changing threat landscape within the IoT space.

5. Regulatory Compliance and Ethical Hacking: Aligning with Cybersecurity Standards

a. Adherence to Cybersecurity Standards: Navigating the Regulatory Tapestry

The regulatory tapestry in the IoT industry is woven with evolving cybersecurity standards and regulations. Ethical hacking becomes a guiding compass for organizations, assisting them in navigating this intricate landscape with adherence to these standards. This collaborative effort ensures that IoT devices not only meet but exceed the cybersecurity benchmarks set by regulatory bodies.

Ethical hackers, well-versed in the nuances of cybersecurity standards, collaborate with organizations to implement security measures that align with these regulations. Whether it's data encryption, access control, or secure communication protocols, the collaborative approach ensures that IoT devices stand resilient in the face of regulatory scrutiny. Adherence to these standards fosters a culture of proactive security and risk management within the IoT ecosystem.

b. Demonstrating Due Diligence: Proactive Trust-building

Engaging in ethical hacking is not merely a regulatory checkbox; it's a proactive stance that organizations take to demonstrate due diligence in securing IoT devices and networks. This collaborative endeavor is a crucial factor in building trust not only with regulatory authorities but also with users, customers, and stakeholders.

By actively involving ethical hackers in the security posture, organizations signal a commitment to transparency and accountability. This proactive trust-building extends beyond compliance; it becomes a strategic asset in the competitive landscape of the IoT industry. Users and customers, reassured by the demonstrated commitment to security, are more likely to trust and adopt IoT technologies.

6. Ethical Hacking Challenges in the IoT Space: Navigating Complexity

a. Diverse Ecosystems and Protocols: A Tapestry of Complexity

The IoT ecosystem is a tapestry woven with diversity, encompassing a myriad of devices, communication protocols, and applications. Ethical hackers, tasked with uncovering vulnerabilities effectively, face the challenge of understanding and assessing this intricate diversity.

In this movement, ethical hackers adapt their methodologies to navigate the complexities of smart homes, industrial IoT deployments, healthcare systems, and more. The challenge lies not only in identifying vulnerabilities but in comprehending the unique intricacies of each ecosystem. This adaptability is a hallmark of ethical hacking in the diverse and dynamic IoT landscape.

b. Resource Constraints in IoT Devices: Balancing Security and Feasibility

Many IoT devices operate within resource constraints, limiting the feasibility of traditional security measures. Ethical hackers, facing this challenge head-on, must adapt their methodologies to ensure robust security without unduly burdening resource-constrained devices.

The approach involves a delicate balance, where ethical hackers devise security measures that are effective yet mindful of the limitations imposed by device resources. Whether it's optimizing encryption algorithms or implementing lightweight security protocols, the collaborative effort focuses on enhancing security without compromising the functionality of resource-constrained IoT devices.

Conclusion: A Symbiotic Harmony in Ethical Hacking Collaboration

In the grand symphony of securing the IoT landscape, the collaborative approach with ethical hacking takes center stage. Partnerships with manufacturers and developers, continuous testing, regulatory compliance, and addressing the challenges of diverse ecosystems form a symbiotic harmony. Ethical hackers, collaborating with stakeholders, orchestrate a strategic defense that not only aligns with regulatory standards but also fosters trust, adaptability, and resilience within the dynamic IoT ecosystem.

7. The Future of Ethical Hacking in IoT Security: A Technological Odyssey

a. Integration of Artificial Intelligence (AI) and Machine Learning (ML): A Technological Synergy

The future of ethical hacking in the dynamic realm of the Internet of Things (IoT) is on the cusp of a technological revolution. At the forefront of this revolution is the integration of Artificial Intelligence (AI) and Machine Learning (ML) technologies. This transformative marriage of technology promises to redefine the landscape of ethical hacking in the IoT space, ushering in an era of enhanced vulnerability detection, streamlined automation of repetitive tasks, and real-time analysis of vast datasets to identify emerging threats.

Enhanced Vulnerability Detection:

AI and ML algorithms, driven by their capacity to learn and adapt, hold the key to revolutionizing vulnerability detection in IoT devices. Ethical hackers, armed with these advanced technologies, can unleash a new era of precision in identifying potential weaknesses. The algorithms can analyze historical data, understand evolving attack patterns, and proactively identify vulnerabilities that may have eluded traditional methods.

Automation of Repetitive Tasks:

The integration of AI and ML brings with it the promise of automating repetitive tasks inherent in ethical hacking. Mundane and time-consuming activities, such as routine scans and pattern recognition, can be delegated to

116

intelligent algorithms. This not only accelerates the ethical hacking process but also allows human ethical hackers to focus on more strategic and nuanced aspects of security assessments.

Real-time Analysis of Emerging Threats:

The dynamic nature of the IoT landscape demands real-time insights into emerging threats. AI and ML technologies excel in analyzing vast datasets at remarkable speeds, enabling ethical hackers to identify and respond to emerging threats in real time. The predictive capabilities of these technologies provide a proactive defense mechanism, staying ahead of the ever-evolving threat landscape within the IoT space.

b. Expansion of Bug Bounty Programs: A Community-Driven Defense

Bug bounty programs, a beacon of collaborative security in the digital landscape, are poised for expansion within the IoT industry. This collaborative model incentivizes ethical hackers to actively participate in discovering and reporting vulnerabilities, fostering a community-driven approach to security.

Incentivizing Ethical Hacking:

Bug bounty programs offer tangible incentives to ethical hackers for responsibly disclosing vulnerabilities. This collaborative model creates a symbiotic relationship where ethical hackers contribute their expertise, and organizations reciprocate with rewards. The expansion of bug bounty programs in the IoT space not only widens the pool of security researchers but also enhances the collective defense against potential threats.

Community-Driven Security:

117

The community-driven nature of bug bounty programs fosters a sense of shared responsibility for IoT security. Ethical hackers, spanning diverse backgrounds and expertise, become integral contributors to the overall security posture. The collective intelligence of the ethical hacking community serves as a powerful defense against the ever-present and evolving threats within the IoT landscape.

Conclusion: Safeguarding the Digital Nexus with Ethical Hacking

In conclusion, ethical hacking stands as a formidable ally in safeguarding the ever-expanding digital nexus of the Internet of Things. As the promise of a connected and convenient IoT world continues to unfold, the proactive efforts of ethical hackers become indispensable in identifying and mitigating vulnerabilities before they can be exploited for malicious purposes.

A Collaborative Approach:

Ethical hacking, embracing a collaborative approach, not only involves partnerships with manufacturers and developers but also extends to bug bounty programs that incentivize a community-driven defense. This collaborative synergy ensures that diverse perspectives and expertise contribute to the resilience of the IoT ecosystem.

Continuous Testing and Adaptability:

The future of ethical hacking in IoT security hinges on continuous testing and adaptability. With the integration of AI and ML technologies, ethical hackers are poised to navigate the dynamic threat landscape with precision, automating routine tasks and gaining real-time insights into emerging threats.

Technological Odyssey:

The integration of AI and ML technologies represents a technological odyssey that propels ethical hacking into a new era of efficacy and sophistication. The expansion of bug bounty programs, driven by a community-driven ethos, reinforces the collective defense against potential threats, creating a robust security posture for the interconnected IoT world.

The role of penetration testing in identifying vulnerabilities in IoT devices and networks

The proliferation of Internet of Things (IoT) devices has ushered in an era of unprecedented connectivity and convenience. From smart homes to industrial environments, the seamless integration of IoT devices has become an integral part of our daily lives. However, this interconnected landscape also brings forth significant cybersecurity challenges, as each connected device represents a potential entry point for malicious actors. In this complex ecosystem, the role of penetration testing emerges as a critical strategy for identifying vulnerabilities and fortifying the security posture of IoT devices and networks.

Understanding Penetration Testing: Unveiling Vulnerabilities Strategically

Penetration testing, often referred to as ethical hacking or "pen testing," is a proactive cybersecurity approach aimed at identifying and exploiting vulnerabilities in a system, network, or application. In the context of IoT devices and networks, penetration testing becomes a strategic imperative to assess the robustness of security measures and uncover potential weaknesses that could be exploited by cyber adversaries.

I. The Landscape of IoT Security Challenges

a. Diverse Ecosystems and Protocols: The Complexity Conundrum

The IoT landscape is characterized by a diverse array of devices, each with its unique functionalities, communication protocols, and security implementations. From smart thermostats to industrial sensors, the sheer variety of devices adds complexity to the security landscape. Penetration testing navigates this complexity by adopting a comprehensive approach that mirrors the diversity of the IoT ecosystem.

b. Resource Constraints: Balancing Security and Functionality

Many IoT devices operate with resource constraints, limiting the feasibility of traditional security measures. Penetration testing in this context involves a delicate balance, where ethical hackers emulate real-world attack scenarios while considering the resource limitations of the targeted devices. This approach ensures that security measures are effective without compromising the functionality of resource-constrained IoT devices.

II. The Strategic Role of Penetration Testing in IoT Security

a. Identifying Weaknesses in Device Implementations

Penetration testing delves into the specific implementations of security measures on IoT devices. Ethical hackers simulate various attack scenarios, attempting to exploit vulnerabilities that may arise from inadequate encryption, weak authentication mechanisms, or insecure firmware. By scrutinizing the device's security posture, penetration testing identifies weaknesses that could be leveraged by malicious actors.

b. Assessing Communication Protocols: Unveiling Network Vulnerabilities

Communication networks, such as the Controller Area Network (CAN), Local Interconnect Network (LIN), and Ethernet, serve as the lifeblood of IoT ecosystems. Penetration testing focuses on these communication protocols, assessing their vulnerability to interception, manipulation, or unauthorized access. By emulating attacks on communication channels, penetration testing reveals potential weaknesses in the network architecture.

III. Methodologies and Approaches in Penetration Testing for IoT

a. Reconnaissance and Information Gathering: Understanding the IoT Landscape

The initial phase of penetration testing involves reconnaissance, where ethical hackers strive to understand the intricacies of the targeted IoT landscape. This includes identifying devices, mapping communication protocols, and discerning potential entry points. In the context of IoT, where diversity is paramount, reconnaissance lays the foundation for a nuanced and effective penetration testing strategy.

b. Vulnerability Assessment: Unveiling Weaknesses

Building on reconnaissance, penetration testing proceeds to a comprehensive vulnerability assessment. This phase involves identifying weaknesses, misconfigurations, and potential entry points within the IoT ecosystem. By systematically probing the devices and networks, ethical hackers uncover vulnerabilities that may have been overlooked in traditional security assessments.

121

c. Exploitation and Simulation of Attacks: Mirroring Real-world Threats

The core of penetration testing lies in the exploitation and simulation of real-world attacks. Ethical hackers, armed with the insights gained from reconnaissance and vulnerability assessment, attempt to exploit identified weaknesses. This may include unauthorized access, manipulation of data, or compromise of IoT device functionalities. By emulating the tactics of malicious actors, penetration testing provides a realistic assessment of the potential impact of security breaches.

d. Post-Exploitation Analysis: Deciphering the Aftermath

After simulating attacks, penetration testing involves a meticulous analysis of the aftermath. Ethical hackers scrutinize the data, patterns, and consequences of their actions. This post-exploitation analysis is crucial for understanding the potential impact of a security breach and devising effective remediation strategies. It serves as a feedback loop, informing both ethical hackers and organizations about the effectiveness of existing security measures.

IV. The Evolving Landscape: Integration of AI and ML in Penetration Testing

a. Enhanced Vulnerability Detection: Leveraging Machine Intelligence

The integration of Artificial Intelligence (AI) and Machine Learning (ML) technologies represents the next frontier in penetration testing for IoT security. These technologies enhance vulnerability detection by analyzing vast datasets, learning from historical attack patterns, and adapting to emerging threats in real time. Ethical hackers, armed with

AI and ML capabilities, can identify vulnerabilities with greater precision and efficiency.

b. Automation of Repetitive Tasks: Streamlining Penetration Testing

AI and ML contribute to the automation of repetitive tasks in penetration testing. Mundane activities, such as routine scans and pattern recognition, can be delegated to intelligent algorithms. This not only accelerates the penetration testing process but also allows ethical hackers to focus on more strategic aspects of security assessments. The automation of repetitive tasks ensures a more comprehensive and efficient evaluation of IoT devices and networks.

V. Bug Bounty Programs: Crowdsourcing Security

a. Incentivizing Ethical Hacking: Collaborative Defense

Bug bounty programs, where organizations incentivize ethical hackers to discover and report vulnerabilities, complement traditional penetration testing approaches. This collaborative model encourages a community-driven approach to security. Ethical hackers, motivated by rewards and recognition, actively contribute to identifying vulnerabilities in IoT devices and networks.

b. Community-Driven Security: Harnessing Collective Intelligence

Bug bounty programs foster a sense of shared responsibility for IoT security. Ethical hackers from diverse backgrounds and expertise become integral contributors to the overall security posture. The collective intelligence of the ethical hacking community serves as a powerful defense against the ever-present and evolving threats within the IoT landscape.

VI. Challenges and Considerations in Penetration Testing for IoT

a. Diverse Ecosystems and Protocols: Navigating Complexity

The diverse nature of IoT ecosystems poses a challenge for penetration testing. Ethical hackers must adapt their methodologies to understand and assess the intricacies of smart homes, industrial IoT deployments, healthcare systems, and more. Navigating this complexity requires a nuanced and tailored approach to penetration testing.

b. Resource Constraints in IoT Devices: Balancing Security and Feasibility

Resource constraints in many IoT devices present a challenge for penetration testing. Ethical hackers must adapt their methodologies to account for these limitations while ensuring robust security. Striking a balance between security and feasibility becomes paramount in the context of resource-constrained IoT devices.

VII. The Future of Penetration Testing in IoT Security

a. Integration of AI and ML: A Transformative Paradigm

The future of penetration testing in IoT security is intrinsically tied to the integration of AI and ML technologies. These technologies represent a transformative paradigm, enhancing the precision and efficiency of vulnerability detection. Ethical hackers, equipped with AI and ML capabilities, will navigate the evolving IoT landscape with unparalleled insights and adaptability.

b. Expansion of Bug Bounty Programs: Strengthening Collaborative Defense

Bug bounty programs will continue to play a pivotal role in the future of penetration testing for IoT security. The expansion of these programs will further strengthen the collaborative defense against emerging threats. Incentivizing ethical hacking on a global scale ensures a diverse pool of talent actively contributing to the security resilience of IoT ecosystems.

Conclusion: Safeguarding the IoT Ecosystem Through Strategic Penetration Testing

In conclusion, penetration testing stands as a linchpin in safeguarding the IoT ecosystem. As the interconnected web of devices continues to expand, the strategic role of ethical hacking becomes indispensable. Penetration testing, encompassing diverse methodologies, approaches, and technologies, serves as a proactive defense against potential vulnerabilities. From uncovering weaknesses in device implementations to assessing network vulnerabilities and embracing the transformative power of AI and ML, penetration testing ensures that IoT devices and networks are resilient against evolving cybersecurity threats.

Responsible disclosure practices in the IoT ecosystem

The rapid proliferation of Internet of Things (IoT) devices has ushered in unprecedented connectivity and convenience across diverse domains, from smart homes to industrial settings. However, this interconnected landscape brings forth significant cybersecurity challenges, necessitating a proactive and responsible approach. Ethical hacking in the IoT space plays a pivotal role, not only in identifying vulnerabilities but also in ensuring the responsible disclosure of these findings. This exploration delves into the significance of responsible disclosure practices, emphasizing their crucial role in maintaining a delicate balance between security transparency and mitigating potential risks.

I. The Ethical Hacker's Dilemma: Navigating Transparency and Security

a. The Dual Role of Ethical Hackers: Guardians and Disclosers

Ethical hackers, also known as white-hat hackers, assume a dual role as guardians of cybersecurity and disclosers of vulnerabilities. Their mission involves proactively identifying weaknesses in IoT devices and networks to fortify security. However, the responsibility doesn't end with discovery; it extends to how these findings are communicated and addressed.

b. The Delicate Balance: Transparency vs. Security Impact

Responsible disclosure practices entail striking a delicate balance between transparency and minimizing the potential impact on security. Ethical hackers walk a fine line, ensuring that the public, manufacturers, and users are informed about vulnerabilities without inadvertently aiding malicious actors.

II. The Anatomy of Responsible Disclosure Practices

a. Timely Notification: Mitigating Security Risks

Timely notification is a cornerstone of responsible disclosure. Ethical hackers, upon identifying vulnerabilities, prioritize notifying the relevant stakeholders promptly. This proactive approach allows manufacturers to initiate timely patches or updates, mitigating potential security risks before they can be exploited.

b. Private Disclosures to Manufacturers: Collaborative Remediation

Responsible disclosure often involves private communications with manufacturers before public disclosure. Ethical hackers engage in a collaborative dialogue, sharing detailed information about the vulnerabilities with the manufacturers. This collaborative remediation process ensures that security patches can be developed and deployed effectively.

c. Setting Reasonable Timelines: Balancing Urgency and Preparedness

Ethical hackers, in adherence to responsible disclosure practices, set reasonable timelines for manufacturers to address identified vulnerabilities. This balance is critical, as urgent patches are necessary to protect users, but manufacturers also need adequate time to develop robust and thoroughly tested solutions.

d. Coordination with Industry Certifications: Strengthening Security Standards

Responsible disclosure often involves coordination with industry certifications and security organizations. Ethical hackers contribute to strengthening security standards by collaborating with these entities, fostering a collective commitment to cybersecurity within the IoT ecosystem.

III. Challenges in Responsible Disclosure Practices for IoT Security

a. Fragmented Ecosystems: Navigating Diverse Manufacturers

The diverse landscape of IoT devices translates into a multitude of manufacturers, each with unique processes and timelines for addressing vulnerabilities. Ethical hackers encounter challenges in navigating this fragmented ecosystem, requiring adaptability and tailored communication strategies.

b. Resource Constraints in Manufacturers: Recognizing Limitations

127

Some manufacturers, particularly smaller entities, may face resource constraints in promptly addressing identified vulnerabilities. Ethical hackers need to recognize these limitations while advocating for a swift and effective resolution.

c. Public Interest vs. Security Risks: Balancing Stakeholder Interests

Balancing the interests of the public, manufacturers, and security remains a challenge in responsible disclosure. Ethical hackers must carefully assess the potential impact on user safety while advocating for transparency and remediation.

IV. The Collaborative Nature of Responsible Disclosure

a. Bug Bounty Programs: Incentivizing Responsible Disclosure

Bug bounty programs, where manufacturers incentivize ethical hackers to report vulnerabilities, exemplify a collaborative approach to responsible disclosure. These programs create a symbiotic relationship, encouraging ethical hackers to responsibly disclose findings in exchange for recognition and rewards.

b. Public Awareness Campaigns: Empowering Users

Responsible disclosure extends beyond manufacturers to include public awareness campaigns. Ethical hackers engage in educating users about the importance of timely updates and security measures, empowering them to take an active role in securing their IoT devices.

V. Legal and Ethical Considerations in Responsible Disclosure

a. Navigating Legal Frameworks: Ensuring Compliance

Ethical hackers must navigate legal frameworks governing responsible disclosure. Understanding the legal landscape ensures that their actions align with established norms, protecting them from unintended legal consequences.

b. Ethical Considerations: Upholding Integrity

Ethical considerations are at the core of responsible disclosure. Ethical hackers prioritize transparency, integrity, and the well-being of users, ensuring that their actions contribute to a safer and more secure IoT ecosystem.

VI. The Future Landscape of Responsible Disclosure in IoT Security

a. International Standards and Collaborations: Unifying Practices

The future of responsible disclosure in IoT security involves the development of international standards and collaborations. Ethical hackers, alongside manufacturers and regulatory bodies, contribute to the establishment of unified practices that transcend geographical boundaries.

b. Technological Solutions: Automated Remediation

Advancements in technology may lead to automated remediation solutions. Ethical hackers may collaborate with manufacturers to develop automated patches or updates, streamlining the responsible disclosure process and reducing the time between identification and resolution.

VII. Conclusion: The Ethical Imperative of Responsible Disclosure

Responsible disclosure practices in the IoT space are not just a matter of protocol; they represent an ethical imperative. Ethical hackers, as stewards of cybersecurity, play a pivotal role in maintaining the delicate balance between transparency and security impact. Navigating the complexities of diverse ecosystems, resource constraints, legal considerations, and ethical principles, they contribute to building a safer and more resilient IoT landscape.

9. IoT Security Best Practices

Comprehensive set of best practices for securing IoT deployment

The Internet of Things (IoT) has transformed the way we interact with the digital world, connecting devices and systems to enhance efficiency and convenience. However, this interconnected landscape brings forth unprecedented security challenges. Securing IoT deployments is imperative to protect against potential cyber threats and ensure the integrity of connected systems. This comprehensive set of best practices outlines key strategies and measures to safeguard IoT deployments.

I. Device Security Best Practices

a. Implement Strong Authentication: The First Line of Defense

Ensuring that devices are protected by robust authentication mechanisms is fundamental. Utilize multi-factor authentication (MFA) to add an extra layer of security beyond traditional passwords, reducing the risk of unauthorized access.

b. Regular Software Updates and Patch Management: Fortifying Defenses

Frequently update device firmware and software to patch known vulnerabilities. Establish a systematic approach to manage updates efficiently, minimizing the window of opportunity for potential exploits.

c. Secure Boot Processes: Guarding Against Unauthorized Access

Incorporate secure boot processes to verify the integrity of device software during startup. This prevents the execution of compromised or unauthorized code, establishing a secure foundation for device operations.

d. Device Identity Management: Establishing Trust

Implement a robust device identity management system to verify and authenticate devices within the IoT network. This ensures that only authorized and legitimate devices can participate in data exchanges.

II. Network Security Best Practices

a. Encrypt Communication Channels: Protecting Data in Transit

Employ strong encryption protocols to safeguard data transmitted between IoT devices and networks. This mitigates the risk of eavesdropping and unauthorized access to sensitive information.

b. Implement Network Segmentation: Restricting Lateral Movement

Divide the IoT network into segments to limit the potential impact of a security breach. Network segmentation prevents unauthorized lateral movement, containing security incidents to specific segments.

c. Network Monitoring and Intrusion Detection: Early Threat Detection

Deploy robust network monitoring tools and intrusion detection systems to detect unusual activities or anomalies. Early detection enables prompt response to potential security threats, minimizing the impact of attacks.

d. Firewall Protection: Defending Entry Points

Utilize firewalls to control and monitor incoming and outgoing traffic. Firewalls act as a barrier against unauthorized access, scrutinizing data packets to ensure that only legitimate communications are allowed.

III. Data Security Best Practices

a. Data Encryption at Rest: Securing Stored Information
Encrypt data when it is stored on devices or servers. This adds an extra layer of protection, ensuring that even if physical access is gained, the data remains unintelligible without the appropriate decryption keys.
b. Data Integrity Checks: Ensuring Information Accuracy
Implement data integrity checks to verify the accuracy and consistency of information throughout its lifecycle. This guards against data tampering and ensures the reliability of IoT-generated data.
c. Role-Based Access Control: Restricting Data Access
Employ role-based access control mechanisms to manage and restrict user access to IoT data. This ensures that individuals or systems only access information relevant to their specific roles and responsibilities.
d. Privacy by Design: Embedding Privacy Measures
Incorporate privacy considerations into the design and development of IoT systems. Prioritize data minimization, anonymization, and user consent to uphold privacy standards from the inception of the IoT deployment.
IV. Physical Security Best Practices
a. Device and Infrastructure Protection: Guarding Against Tampering
Implement physical security measures to protect IoT devices and infrastructure from tampering or theft. This includes secure housing, access controls, and tamper-evident technologies.
b. Supply Chain Security: Verifying Component Integrity
Ensure the integrity of the supply chain by validating the security of components and devices throughout the manufacturing process. This mitigates the risk of

incorporating compromised or malicious components into the IoT ecosystem.

c. Secure Disposal and Decommissioning: Preventing Data Leakage

Establish secure procedures for decommissioning and disposing of IoT devices. This prevents data leakage and ensures that sensitive information is permanently erased from retired devices.

V. Policy and Governance Best Practices

a. Establish a Comprehensive Security Policy: Setting Guidelines

Develop and enforce a comprehensive security policy that outlines guidelines and best practices for IoT security. This policy should encompass device management, network protocols, data handling, and user access controls.

b. Regular Security Audits and Assessments: Continuous Improvement

Conduct regular security audits and assessments to evaluate the effectiveness of security controls. Identify vulnerabilities and weaknesses, enabling continuous improvement of IoT security measures.

c. Incident Response Plan: Readiness for Security Incidents

Develop and regularly update an incident response plan to ensure a swift and coordinated response to security incidents. This plan should outline roles, responsibilities, and steps to be taken in the event of a breach.

d. Employee Training and Awareness: Building a Security Culture

Educate employees and stakeholders about IoT security risks and best practices. Foster a security-conscious culture, emphasizing the importance of individual contributions to overall cybersecurity.

VI. Regulatory Compliance Best Practices

a. Adherence to Data Protection Regulations: Legal Compliance

Ensure compliance with relevant data protection regulations and standards, such as GDPR, HIPAA, or industry-specific requirements. Adhering to regulatory frameworks is essential for legal compliance and maintaining trust.

b. Transparent Privacy Policies: User Communication

Maintain transparent privacy policies that clearly communicate how IoT data is collected, processed, and shared. Providing users with clear information enhances trust and ensures compliance with privacy regulations.

VII. Collaboration and Information Sharing

a. Participation in Information Sharing Initiatives: Strengthening Collective Security

Participate in information-sharing initiatives and collaborate with industry peers to share insights and threat intelligence. This collective approach strengthens the overall security posture of the IoT ecosystem.

b. Engagement with Security Communities: Continuous Learning

Engage with security communities, forums, and conferences to stay informed about the latest threats and security best practices. Continuous learning and collaboration contribute to a dynamic and adaptive security strategy.

VIII. Emerging Technologies and Future Considerations

a. Blockchain for Enhanced Security: Decentralized Trust

Explore the potential of blockchain technology to enhance security in IoT deployments. Blockchain offers decentralized and tamper-resistant ledger capabilities, providing a secure foundation for IoT transactions.

b. Artificial Intelligence for Threat Detection: Proactive Security

Integrate artificial intelligence (AI) into security systems to enable proactive threat detection. AI algorithms can analyze patterns, detect anomalies, and respond to potential threats in real-time.

IX. Conclusion: Ensuring the Resilience of IoT Deployments

Securing IoT deployments requires a holistic and proactive approach that encompasses device, network, data, physical, policy, and regulatory considerations. By adopting these comprehensive best practices, organizations can fortify the resilience of their IoT ecosystems, mitigating potential risks and ensuring the continued trust of users and stakeholders.

IoT Security Best Practices: device management, secure coding practices, and ongoing monitoring

The proliferation of Internet of Things (IoT) devices has introduced unparalleled convenience and efficiency across various industries. However, this interconnected landscape also poses significant security challenges. This comprehensive guide outlines best practices for IoT security, focusing on critical aspects such as device management, secure coding practices, and ongoing monitoring.

I. Device Management Best Practices

a. Inventory and Asset Management: Know Your Devices
Maintain a comprehensive inventory of all IoT devices within your network. This includes details such as device types, manufacturers, firmware versions, and associated IP addresses. Regularly update this inventory to reflect changes in the device landscape.
b. Authentication and Authorization: Strengthen Access Controls
Implement robust authentication mechanisms to ensure that only authorized personnel can access and manage IoT devices. Utilize strong, unique passwords and consider multi-factor authentication for an additional layer of security.
c. Remote Management Security: Balancing Convenience and Risk
If remote management is necessary, ensure that these capabilities are secure. Use encrypted communication channels and employ secure protocols to prevent unauthorized access to devices, balancing the convenience of remote management with security considerations.
d. Firmware and Software Updates: Timely Patching
Establish a systematic approach to firmware and software updates. Regularly check for updates from manufacturers and apply patches promptly to address known vulnerabilities. Automated update mechanisms can streamline this process.
II. Secure Coding Practices for IoT
a. Input Validation: Guarding Against Injection Attacks
Implement rigorous input validation mechanisms in IoT device software. This guards against injection attacks by ensuring that only valid and expected data is processed, preventing malicious input from compromising the system.

b. Encryption for Data in Transit and at Rest: Protecting Confidentiality

Incorporate encryption for both data in transit and at rest. This safeguards sensitive information from interception during transmission and ensures that stored data remains secure even if physical access to the device is gained.

c. Least Privilege Principle: Restricting Access

Follow the principle of least privilege when defining user and application permissions. Limit access rights to only those necessary for the proper functioning of the device, reducing the potential impact of a security breach.

d. Error Handling: Providing Secure Feedback

Implement secure error handling mechanisms to prevent the disclosure of sensitive information in error messages. Provide generic error messages to users and log detailed error information internally for analysis.

e. Secure Protocols for Communication: Choosing Wisely

Select secure communication protocols for IoT devices. Avoid insecure protocols and prioritize those with encryption capabilities, ensuring the confidentiality and integrity of data exchanged between devices and networks.

III. Ongoing Monitoring Best Practices

a. Network Traffic Analysis: Identifying Anomalies

Regularly analyze network traffic to identify anomalies or suspicious activities. Implement intrusion detection systems (IDS) and intrusion prevention systems (IPS) to automatically respond to potential threats in real-time.

b. Behavioral Analysis: Understanding Normal Patterns

Employ behavioral analysis tools to understand normal patterns of IoT device behavior. Deviations from established baselines can indicate potential security incidents, prompting timely investigation and response.

c. Incident Response Planning: Ready for Action
Develop and regularly update an incident response plan specifically tailored for IoT security incidents. Clearly outline roles, responsibilities, and escalation procedures to ensure a swift and coordinated response when a security event occurs.

d. Continuous Security Auditing: Identifying Weaknesses
Conduct regular security audits to identify weaknesses in the IoT security infrastructure. This proactive approach enables organizations to address vulnerabilities before they can be exploited.

e. User Activity Monitoring: Detecting Anomalous Behavior
Implement user activity monitoring to detect anomalous behavior that may indicate unauthorized access or misuse of IoT devices. This includes tracking user logins, access patterns, and changes to device configurations.

IV. Integration of Best Practices: A Holistic Approach
a. Holistic Security Policies: Coordinated Measures
Integrate device management, secure coding practices, and ongoing monitoring into holistic security policies. These policies should encompass all aspects of IoT security, providing a coordinated framework for effective risk management.

b. Employee Training: Fostering a Security Culture
Educate employees about the importance of following secure coding practices, adhering to device management protocols, and participating in ongoing monitoring efforts. Fostering a security-conscious culture is crucial for the success of these measures.

c. Collaboration Across Teams: Breaking Silos
Encourage collaboration between device management, development, and security teams. Breaking silos and

fostering cross-functional collaboration ensures that security considerations are integrated into the entire IoT lifecycle.

V. Challenges and Considerations in Implementing Best Practices

a. Resource Constraints: Balancing Security and Functionality

Many IoT devices operate with resource constraints, limiting the feasibility of certain security measures. Organizations must strike a balance between security and functionality, adapting best practices to the specific capabilities of their devices.

b. Diversity of IoT Ecosystems: Tailoring Approaches

The diversity of IoT ecosystems presents a challenge in implementing standardized best practices. Organizations should tailor their approaches to accommodate the unique characteristics of their specific IoT deployments.

c. Regulatory Compliance: Navigating Legal Frameworks

Navigate the legal landscape and ensure that IoT deployments comply with relevant data protection and privacy regulations. Understanding and adhering to regulatory frameworks is essential for legal compliance.

VI. Conclusion: Building a Robust Foundation for IoT Security

In conclusion, securing IoT deployments requires a multifaceted approach that encompasses device management, secure coding practices, and ongoing monitoring. By implementing these best practices, organizations can build a robust foundation for IoT security, mitigating risks and ensuring the resilience of their interconnected ecosystems.

IoT Security Best Practices: practical tips for both manufacturers and end-users

The rapid expansion of the Internet of Things (IoT) has introduced a multitude of interconnected devices, bringing convenience and efficiency to our daily lives. However, this connectivity also raises significant security concerns. This practical guide outlines IoT security best practices, offering actionable tips for both manufacturers and end-users to enhance the security posture of IoT deployments.

I. For Manufacturers: Building Secure Foundations

a. Secure-by-Design Principles: Prioritize Security from Inception

Tip for Manufacturers: Embed security considerations into the design phase of IoT devices. Prioritize security features and considerations right from the inception of the device development process.

b. Thorough Device Testing: Rigorous Quality Assurance

Tip for Manufacturers: Conduct thorough testing and quality assurance processes for IoT devices. Identify and address vulnerabilities before devices reach the market to ensure a robust security posture.

c. Regular Security Updates: Post-Deployment Vigilance

Tip for Manufacturers: Establish mechanisms for regular security updates post-deployment. Provide ongoing support to address emerging threats and vulnerabilities, demonstrating a commitment to long-term device security.

d. Transparency in Data Handling: Clear Communication with Users

Tip for Manufacturers: Clearly communicate data handling practices to users. Establish transparent privacy policies, detailing how user data is collected, processed, and shared, building trust through clear communication.

II. For End-Users: Navigating the IoT Security Landscape

a. Change Default Credentials: Strengthening Device Access

Tip for End-Users: Change default usernames and passwords on IoT devices. Strengthen device access controls by using unique, strong credentials to prevent unauthorized access.

b. Regular Firmware Updates: Keeping Devices Current

Tip for End-Users: Regularly update firmware on IoT devices. Enable automatic updates when possible, ensuring that devices benefit from the latest security patches and enhancements.

c. Network Segmentation: Isolating IoT Devices

Tip for End-Users: Implement network segmentation to isolate IoT devices from critical systems. This prevents unauthorized access and limits the potential impact of a security breach.

d. Monitor Device Behavior: Identifying Anomalies

Tip for End-Users: Monitor the behavior of IoT devices. Be vigilant for any unusual activities or behaviors that may indicate a security incident, prompting timely investigation.

III. For Manufacturers: Secure Communication Protocols

a. Use of Encrypted Channels: Protecting Data in Transit

Tip for Manufacturers: Implement encrypted communication channels for IoT devices. Prioritize the use of secure protocols to protect data in transit and mitigate the risk of unauthorized access.

b. Authentication Mechanisms: Multi-Factor Security

Tip for Manufacturers: Integrate robust authentication mechanisms. Consider multi-factor authentication to add an additional layer of security, requiring users to provide multiple forms of identification.

c. Regular Security Audits: Ongoing Device Evaluation

Tip for Manufacturers: Conduct regular security audits on devices. Continuously evaluate the effectiveness of security measures and address any identified vulnerabilities promptly.

d. Supply Chain Security: Ensuring Component Integrity

Tip for Manufacturers: Ensure the integrity of the supply chain. Verify the security of components throughout the manufacturing process to prevent the inclusion of compromised elements.

IV. For End-Users: User Authentication Practices

a. Secure User Authentication: Strong Passwords

Tip for End-Users: Implement secure authentication practices. Use strong, unique passwords for accessing IoT devices and consider the use of password management tools to enhance security.

b. Review and Understand Privacy Policies: Informed Consent

Tip for End-Users: Review and understand privacy policies associated with IoT devices. Ensure informed consent by being aware of how your data is handled and shared.

c. Regular Security Awareness: Staying Informed

Tip for End-Users: Stay informed about cybersecurity best practices. Regularly update your knowledge on security measures to better protect yourself and your connected devices.

d. Secure Wi-Fi Networks: Protecting Device Communication

Tip for End-Users: Secure your Wi-Fi networks. Implement strong encryption protocols and use unique, strong passwords for your Wi-Fi network to prevent unauthorized access to IoT devices.

V. For Manufacturers: Collaborative Security Initiatives

a. Partnerships for Security: Collaborating with Peers

Tip for Manufacturers: Engage in partnerships and collaborations with other manufacturers. Sharing insights and threat intelligence can strengthen the overall security ecosystem.

b. Bug Bounty Programs: Encouraging Responsible Disclosure

Tip for Manufacturers: Establish bug bounty programs. Encourage ethical hackers to responsibly disclose vulnerabilities by providing incentives for identifying and reporting security issues.

c. Regulatory Compliance: Adhering to Standards

Tip for Manufacturers: Ensure compliance with regulatory standards. Adhering to industry-specific and global regulations fosters a culture of proactive security and risk management.

d. Continuous Security Education: Empowering Development Teams

Tip for Manufacturers: Continuously educate development teams about evolving security threats. Empower them to implement the latest security measures and stay ahead of emerging risks.

VI. For End-Users: Secure Physical Access

a. Secure Device Placement: Preventing Tampering

Tip for End-Users: Secure the physical placement of IoT devices. Prevent tampering or unauthorized access by placing devices in secure locations, especially those with sensitive information.

b. Disposal of Devices: Ensuring Data Erasure

Tip for End-Users: Properly dispose of IoT devices. Ensure that sensitive information is permanently erased from retired devices to prevent data leakage.

c. Report Suspicious Activity: A Community Approach

Tip for End-Users: Report suspicious activity. If you notice unusual behavior from your IoT devices, report it to manufacturers and relevant authorities to contribute to collective security.

d. User Support and Education: Empowering Users

Tip for End-Users: Manufacturers should provide user support and education. Empower users with the knowledge and tools to secure their IoT devices effectively.

10. Future Trends in IoT Security

Explore emerging technologies that could impact the future of IoT security

The Internet of Things (IoT) continues to reshape the way we interact with technology, transforming industries and enhancing our daily lives. However, this rapid expansion also brings forth new and evolving security challenges. To stay ahead of potential threats, it's crucial to explore the future trends in IoT security. This comprehensive exploration delves into emerging technologies that are poised to impact the future of IoT security, providing insights into the evolving landscape.

I. Blockchain Integration: Decentralized Trust

Blockchain technology, known for its decentralized and tamper-resistant characteristics, holds significant promise for enhancing IoT security.

a. Decentralized Security: Immutable Ledgers

Blockchain's decentralized ledger ensures that data transactions are recorded in a tamper-resistant manner. This prevents unauthorized alterations to data, offering a robust foundation for securing the vast amounts of data generated by IoT devices.

b. Secure Device Identity: Public Key Infrastructure (PKI)

Implementing PKI on a blockchain provides a secure foundation for establishing device identities. Each device is assigned a unique cryptographic key, enhancing authentication and ensuring that only authorized devices can participate in the IoT network.

c. Smart Contracts for Automation: Code-Based Security Policies

Smart contracts, self-executing contracts with the terms of the agreement directly written into code, can automate security policies within IoT networks. This ensures that predefined security measures are consistently enforced without manual intervention.

d. Supply Chain Security: Verifiable Provenance

Blockchain's transparent and traceable nature is beneficial for supply chain security. Manufacturers can use blockchain to verify the authenticity and integrity of components, mitigating the risk of compromised elements entering the supply chain.

II. Artificial Intelligence (AI) and Machine Learning (ML): Proactive Threat Detection

AI and ML technologies are poised to revolutionize how we approach IoT security by enabling proactive threat detection and response.

a. Anomaly Detection: Identifying Unusual Patterns

AI algorithms can analyze vast datasets generated by IoT devices, identifying patterns and anomalies that may indicate potential security threats. This proactive approach enables organizations to detect and mitigate threats before they escalate.

b. Behavioral Analysis: Understanding Normal Device Behavior

ML-driven behavioral analysis allows for a deep understanding of normal device behavior. Deviations from established baselines can trigger alerts, prompting timely investigation and response to potential security incidents.

c. Automated Response: Rapid Mitigation

AI-powered systems can automate response actions to security incidents. This includes isolating compromised devices, blocking malicious traffic, or triggering predefined security protocols, reducing the response time to emerging threats.

d. Continuous Learning: Adapting to Evolving Threats

AI and ML systems continuously learn from new data, adapting to evolving threats. This dynamic learning capability enhances the resilience of IoT security measures by staying ahead of emerging attack vectors.

III. 5G Connectivity: Enhanced Speed and Security

The rollout of 5G networks introduces not only faster and more reliable connectivity for IoT devices but also enhanced security features.

a. Low Latency Communication: Real-Time Security Measures

5G's low latency communication enables real-time implementation of security measures. This is crucial for IoT devices that require instant responses to security threats, reducing the window of vulnerability.

b. Network Slicing for Segmentation: Isolating Traffic

5G's network slicing allows for the creation of dedicated, isolated segments for specific types of IoT traffic. This segmentation enhances security by isolating compromised devices from critical systems, limiting the potential impact of a security breach.

c. Improved Device Authentication: Strengthening Access Controls

Enhanced authentication protocols in 5G networks strengthen access controls for IoT devices. This reduces the risk of unauthorized access and ensures that only authenticated devices can connect to the network.

d. Edge Computing Integration: Decentralized Processing

5G networks facilitate the integration of edge computing, allowing data processing to occur closer to the source of data generation. This decentralized approach enhances security by reducing the need for data to travel over long distances, minimizing the risk of interception.

IV. Edge Computing: Decentralized Processing and Reduced Vulnerabilities

Edge computing, the practice of processing data closer to the source, is gaining prominence as a trend that significantly impacts IoT security.

a. Reduced Data Transit: Minimizing Interception Risks

By processing data at the edge, closer to where it's generated, edge computing reduces the need for data to transit over extensive networks. This minimizes the risk of interception, enhancing the overall security of IoT data.

b. Localized Data Processing: Privacy Enhancement

Edge computing enables localized data processing, addressing privacy concerns associated with centralized processing. This ensures that sensitive information remains within specific geographic boundaries, complying with data protection regulations.

c. Faster Response Times: Immediate Security Actions

The proximity of edge computing to IoT devices allows for faster response times to security incidents. Immediate security actions, such as isolating compromised devices, can be taken at the edge, reducing the impact of potential threats.

d. Reduced Dependency on Central Servers: Resilience

Edge computing reduces dependency on central servers, making IoT networks more resilient to server-related vulnerabilities or disruptions. This decentralized approach contributes to a more robust and reliable security infrastructure.

V. Hardware-Based Security: Protecting the Foundation

Hardware-based security measures are emerging as a critical trend to fortify the foundational components of IoT devices.

a. Hardware Security Modules (HSMs): Secure Key Storage

HSMs provide secure storage for cryptographic keys, protecting sensitive information from unauthorized access. Integrating HSMs into IoT devices enhances the overall security of cryptographic operations.

b. Secure Enclaves: Isolated Processing Zones

Secure enclaves create isolated processing zones within the hardware, safeguarding critical operations from external interference. This ensures the integrity and confidentiality of sensitive data processed by IoT devices.

c. Trusted Execution Environments (TEEs): Secure Execution of Code

TEEs provide secure execution environments for code, protecting against tampering and unauthorized access. This ensures that the software running on IoT devices is not compromised by malicious entities.

d. Secure Boot Processes: Ensuring Device Integrity

Implementing secure boot processes ensures that IoT devices only execute trusted and verified firmware. This foundational security measure prevents unauthorized modifications to the device's firmware, protecting against malicious attacks.

VI. Quantum-Safe Cryptography: Preparing for Future Threats

The emergence of quantum computing presents a potential threat to current cryptographic algorithms. Quantum-safe cryptography is a proactive approach to address this future risk.

a. Post-Quantum Cryptography: Resistance to Quantum Attacks

Post-quantum cryptographic algorithms are designed to resist attacks from quantum computers. By adopting quantum-safe cryptography, organizations can future-proof their IoT security measures against the anticipated capabilities of quantum computing.

b. Transition Plans: Phased Implementation

Organizations should develop transition plans to integrate post-quantum cryptographic algorithms gradually. This phased approach ensures that existing IoT deployments can evolve to withstand the cryptographic challenges posed by quantum computing advancements.

c. Research and Standardization: Collaborative Efforts

Ongoing research and standardization efforts in quantum-safe cryptography are crucial for the development of robust algorithms. Collaborative initiatives within the cybersecurity community play a vital role in establishing standardized practices for quantum-resistant security.

VII. Conclusion: Adapting to a Dynamic Future

The future of IoT security is undeniably dynamic, shaped by emerging technologies and evolving threat landscapes. Organizations must remain vigilant, embracing these future trends to fortify their IoT ecosystems against an ever-changing array of security challenges.

Potential advancements in blockchain, artificial intelligence, and edge computing

The landscape of Internet of Things (IoT) security is continually evolving, driven by advancements in key technologies. This discussion delves into the potential advancements in three crucial areas—blockchain, artificial intelligence (AI), and edge computing—and their collective impact on the future of IoT security.

I. Blockchain Advancements: Fortifying Trust and Integrity

Blockchain, initially recognized for its role in cryptocurrency, has transcended its origins to become a cornerstone for ensuring trust and integrity in various applications. In the realm of IoT security, several potential advancements are on the horizon.

a. Enhanced Decentralization: Strengthening Data Immutability

Advancements in blockchain technology are expected to enhance decentralization, further strengthening the immutability of data. The distributed nature of blockchain ensures that data recorded in a block is resistant to tampering, providing a robust foundation for securing the vast amounts of data generated by IoT devices.

b. Smart Contracts Evolution: Automating Complex Security Protocols

The evolution of smart contracts within blockchain systems holds the potential to automate complex security protocols in IoT networks. These self-executing contracts, encoded with predefined security measures, can streamline and enhance the enforcement of security policies across interconnected devices.

c. Interoperability Standards: Facilitating Cross-Platform Security

Advancements in blockchain may lead to the establishment of interoperability standards. This is crucial for IoT devices from diverse manufacturers to communicate securely. Blockchain's transparent and standardized approach can facilitate seamless communication, ensuring a consistent and secure flow of data.

d. Scalability Solutions: Addressing Growing IoT Networks

Blockchain's scalability has been a point of consideration for its broader adoption in large-scale IoT networks. Advancements in scalability solutions, such as sharding or layer-two protocols, could address the challenge of accommodating the increasing number of connected devices without compromising on security.

II. Artificial Intelligence Advancements: Proactive Threat Mitigation

Artificial Intelligence (AI) continues to redefine how organizations approach IoT security, offering proactive threat mitigation capabilities. Anticipated advancements in AI for IoT security include:

a. Adaptive Learning Models: Real-Time Threat Identification

Advancements in AI will likely lead to more adaptive learning models capable of real-time threat identification. These models can continuously evolve and learn from new data, enabling them to recognize and mitigate emerging threats with greater accuracy.

b. Autonomous Response Systems: Rapid Countermeasures

The integration of AI into IoT security may result in the development of autonomous response systems. These systems can autonomously execute countermeasures, such as isolating compromised devices or adjusting security configurations, in response to identified threats, reducing response times.

c. Explainable AI: Enhancing Transparency

Explainable AI, a trend gaining prominence, focuses on making AI algorithms more understandable and transparent. In the context of IoT security, this advancement can enhance trust by providing clear explanations of how AI systems arrive at their security-related decisions.

d. Federated Learning: Collaborative Threat Intelligence

Federated learning, where AI models are trained collaboratively across decentralized devices, can advance threat intelligence in IoT ecosystems. This approach allows devices to learn from each other without sharing sensitive data, creating a collaborative defense against evolving threats.

III. Edge Computing Advancements: Decentralized Security Processing

Edge computing, characterized by decentralized data processing closer to the source, is a pivotal technology shaping the future of IoT security. Anticipated advancements in edge computing include:

a. Improved Processing Capabilities: Handling Increasing Data Loads

Advancements in edge computing hardware will likely lead to improved processing capabilities, enabling devices at the edge to handle increasing data loads without compromising on security. This ensures that security measures can be implemented swiftly and efficiently.

b. Decentralized Security Analytics: Localized Threat Detection

The evolution of edge computing may see the implementation of decentralized security analytics. Localized threat detection at the edge allows for quicker identification of security anomalies without the need to transmit extensive amounts of data to centralized servers.

c. Edge-to-Edge Communication Standards: Streamlining Security Protocols

Advancements in edge-to-edge communication standards can streamline security protocols across interconnected devices. This ensures that security measures are consistently applied, promoting a cohesive and secure network of edge devices.

d. Energy-Efficient Edge Devices: Sustainable Security Measures

Future advancements in edge computing will likely focus on energy-efficient edge devices. Sustainable security measures that prioritize energy consumption will be crucial for ensuring the longevity and effectiveness of security protocols in resource-constrained IoT environments.

IV. Synergy of Advancements: The Convergence of Technologies

The true potential of the future of IoT security lies in the synergy of advancements in blockchain, AI, and edge computing. The convergence of these technologies can unlock new possibilities and address complex security challenges:

a. Blockchain and AI Integration: Securing Decentralized Intelligence

The integration of blockchain and AI can create a secure environment for decentralized intelligence. Blockchain's data integrity complements AI's ability to analyze and respond to threats, forming a symbiotic relationship that enhances the overall security of IoT ecosystems.

b. Edge Computing and Blockchain Collaboration: Decentralized Trust at the Edge

Collaboration between edge computing and blockchain can bring decentralized trust to the edge. By recording critical security events on a blockchain, edge devices can contribute to a tamper-resistant and transparent log of security-related activities.

c. AI-Driven Security Analytics at the Edge: Real-Time Threat Detection

The deployment of AI-driven security analytics at the edge can enable real-time threat detection. This approach leverages AI's analytical capabilities locally, minimizing latency and allowing for immediate responses to security incidents.

d. Holistic Security Orchestration: Seamless Integration of Technologies

The future of IoT security will likely see the development of holistic security orchestration platforms that seamlessly integrate blockchain, AI, and edge computing. These platforms can provide a unified framework for managing security measures across diverse IoT environments.

V. Challenges and Considerations: Navigating Complexity

While the anticipated advancements in blockchain, AI, and edge computing offer immense potential for enhancing IoT security, there are challenges and considerations that must be navigated:

a. Interoperability Challenges: Standardizing Integration Protocols

Ensuring seamless interoperability between blockchain, AI, and edge computing technologies may pose challenges. Standardizing integration protocols and communication formats will be essential for realizing the full potential of these advancements.

b. Security and Privacy Concerns: Balancing Innovation with Safeguards

As technologies advance, there is a continuous need to balance innovation with safeguards for security and privacy. Striking the right balance will be crucial to foster trust among users and ensure responsible deployment of IoT security solutions.

c. Resource Constraints: Optimizing for Efficiency

Resource constraints in IoT environments, especially at the edge, may impact the deployment of advanced security measures. Optimizing solutions for efficiency while maintaining robust security will be a key consideration.

d. Regulatory Compliance: Adapting to Evolving Standards

The evolving nature of IoT security technologies necessitates a proactive approach to regulatory compliance. Adapting to evolving standards and ensuring alignment with regulatory requirements will be paramount.

VI. Conclusion: Charting the Course for Secure IoT

The future of IoT security is intricately linked to the advancements in blockchain, AI, and edge computing. As these technologies continue to evolve, organizations must strategically embrace innovation while addressing the associated challenges. The convergence of blockchain, AI, and edge computing holds the promise of fortifying IoT security, ensuring a resilient and secure connected landscape.

Anticipating of challenges and opportunities as IoT continues to evolve

The Internet of Things (IoT) has rapidly evolved, transforming the way we interact with technology and amplifying the potential for innovation across industries. As IoT continues to expand its reach, the landscape of security faces both challenges and opportunities. This exploration anticipates the future trends, examining the hurdles that need to be overcome and the potential opportunities that lie ahead.

I. Challenges in the Evolving IoT Security Landscape

a. Increased Attack Surface: Expanding Vulnerabilities

The proliferation of IoT devices exponentially expands the attack surface. Each connected device becomes a potential entry point for malicious actors, presenting a formidable challenge in securing a diverse and expansive network of devices.

b. Diversity in Devices and Protocols: Interoperability Struggles

The diversity of IoT devices, each operating on different protocols and standards, poses interoperability challenges. Ensuring seamless communication and standardized security measures across this varied landscape becomes increasingly complex.

c. Resource Constraints: Balancing Security and Efficiency

Many IoT devices operate with resource constraints, including limited processing power and memory. Striking a balance between robust security measures and the efficient operation of resource-constrained devices presents an ongoing challenge.

d. Privacy Concerns: Safeguarding Sensitive Data

The vast amount of data generated by IoT devices raises significant privacy concerns. Safeguarding sensitive information and ensuring compliance with privacy regulations become critical considerations for IoT security strategies.

II. Opportunities for Strengthening IoT Security

a. Blockchain for Immutable Security: Tamper-Resistant Data

Blockchain technology presents an opportunity to establish tamper-resistant and immutable security for IoT data. By leveraging decentralized ledgers, organizations can enhance the integrity of data transactions and build trust in the security of their IoT ecosystems.

b. AI-Driven Threat Detection: Proactive Security Measures

Advancements in artificial intelligence (AI) offer opportunities for proactive threat detection. AI-driven models can analyze vast datasets, identify patterns, and autonomously respond to emerging threats, bolstering the overall security posture of IoT networks.

c. Edge Computing for Localized Security: Immediate Response

Edge computing provides an opportunity for localized security measures. By processing data closer to the source, IoT devices can implement immediate responses to security incidents, reducing the time it takes to detect and mitigate threats.

d. Collaborative Security Initiatives: Shared Threat Intelligence

Collaborative security initiatives can strengthen the collective defense against evolving threats. Sharing threat intelligence and best practices across industries and organizations fosters a community-driven approach to IoT security.

III. Navigating Regulatory and Compliance Landscape

a. Dynamic Regulatory Environment: Adapting to Standards

The regulatory landscape for IoT security is dynamic, with evolving standards and compliance requirements. Organizations have the opportunity to take a proactive approach, staying abreast of regulatory changes and adapting their security measures accordingly.

b. Industry-Specific Standards: Tailoring Security Measures

As different industries adopt IoT technologies, industry-specific standards emerge. Tailoring security measures to meet the unique requirements of specific sectors, such as healthcare or manufacturing, enhances the effectiveness of IoT security strategies.

c. Privacy by Design: Integrating Privacy into IoT Solutions

Privacy by design principles offer an opportunity to integrate privacy considerations into the development of IoT solutions. By prioritizing privacy from the outset, organizations can build trust and compliance into their IoT ecosystems.

IV. Balancing Innovation with Security

a. Rapid Technological Advancements: Adapting to Change

The rapid pace of technological advancements introduces both challenges and opportunities. Organizations must balance the drive for innovation with the need to implement robust security measures, ensuring that new technologies enhance rather than compromise security.

b. Security in Product Development: From Inception to Deployment

Embedding security in the product development lifecycle is an opportunity to create resilient IoT solutions. From the initial design phase to deployment, a security-focused approach ensures that devices are built with robust security features.

c. Continuous Security Education: Empowering Stakeholders

Continuous security education for stakeholders, including developers, users, and decision-makers, presents an opportunity to foster a culture of security awareness. Empowered stakeholders are better equipped to make informed decisions that prioritize security.

V. Emerging Threat Vectors: Preparing for the Unpredictable

a. Sophisticated Cyber Threats: Adaptive Security Measures

As cyber threats become more sophisticated, organizations have the opportunity to implement adaptive security measures. This includes leveraging advanced threat intelligence, machine learning, and behavioral analytics to stay one step ahead of evolving threats.

b. Supply Chain Risks: Strengthening Vendor Relationships

Supply chain vulnerabilities pose a significant threat to IoT security. Strengthening vendor relationships, implementing robust supply chain security practices, and conducting thorough risk assessments contribute to mitigating these risks.

c. Insider Threats: Comprehensive Insider Risk Management

Insider threats, whether intentional or unintentional, require comprehensive insider risk management strategies. This includes monitoring user behavior, implementing access controls, and fostering a culture of security awareness among employees.

VI. International Collaboration: Building Global Resilience

a. Global Threat Landscape: Collaborative Defense Strategies

The interconnected nature of the IoT ecosystem necessitates international collaboration. Building global resilience against cyber threats requires collaborative defense strategies, information sharing, and joint efforts to address emerging challenges.

b. Standardization Across Borders: Harmonizing Security Practices

Harmonizing security practices across borders through international standards fosters a more consistent and robust approach to IoT security. This standardization contributes to a shared understanding of best practices and ensures a higher level of security globally.

c. Cross-Industry Knowledge Sharing: Collective Learning

Cross-industry knowledge sharing offers valuable insights and lessons learned. Organizations can benefit from the experiences of others, applying collective learning to strengthen their own IoT security strategies and adapt to emerging threats.

VII. Conclusion: Forging a Secure Future in IoT

The future of IoT security is dynamic, marked by challenges that demand innovative solutions and opportunities that can be seized for enhanced resilience. Navigating this landscape requires a strategic and collaborative approach, where organizations prioritize security as an integral part of their IoT journey. By embracing advancements in technologies like blockchain and AI, adhering to evolving regulations, and fostering a global culture of security, the IoT ecosystem can forge a secure future.

11. Case Studies and Lessons Learned

Real-world case studies of successful IoT security implementations

In the ever-expanding realm of the Internet of Things (IoT), security is paramount. Real-world case studies provide invaluable insights into successful IoT security implementations, showcasing strategies, challenges overcome, and lessons learned. This analysis explores noteworthy case studies, highlighting key elements that contribute to effective IoT security.

I. Smart Grid Security: A Beacon of Resilience

Case Study 1: Securing the Energy Infrastructure

Overview:

In a large-scale smart grid deployment, a utility company faced the challenge of securing critical energy infrastructure against cyber threats. The implementation of a robust security framework involved:

End-to-End Encryption: Ensuring secure communication between smart meters, sensors, and the central grid through end-to-end encryption.

Anomaly Detection Systems: Integrating advanced anomaly detection systems to identify unusual patterns indicative of potential cyber threats.

Regular Security Audits: Conducting frequent security audits and penetration testing to assess vulnerabilities and address them promptly.

Lessons Learned:

The success of this implementation underscores the importance of a comprehensive security approach, combining encryption, advanced monitoring, and regular assessments. Lessons include:

- Holistic Protection: Implementing security measures across the entire IoT ecosystem, from edge devices to central systems.

- Adaptability: Building systems that can adapt to emerging threats through continuous monitoring and dynamic security updates.

II. Connected Healthcare: Safeguarding Patient Data

Case Study 2: IoT Security in Healthcare Devices

Overview:

A healthcare provider embraced IoT to enhance patient care through connected medical devices. The security implementation focused on safeguarding patient data, featuring:

Data Encryption: Employing robust encryption protocols to protect sensitive patient information transmitted between devices and the central healthcare system.

Access Controls: Implementing strict access controls to ensure that only authorized personnel can interact with and configure medical devices.

Secure Device Lifecycle Management: Incorporating secure device onboarding and decommissioning processes to prevent unauthorized access during the device lifecycle.

Lessons Learned:

This case study highlights the critical nature of security in healthcare IoT, with lessons including:

- Privacy Prioritization: Placing a strong emphasis on patient privacy, ensuring compliance with healthcare data protection regulations.

- End-of-Life Security: Implementing secure decommissioning processes to prevent security vulnerabilities in retired devices.

III. Industrial IoT: Fortifying Operational Technology

Case Study 3: Strengthening Industrial Control Systems (ICS)

Overview:

An industrial facility sought to enhance the security of its Industrial Control Systems (ICS) using IoT technologies. Key security measures included:

Network Segmentation: Implementing robust network segmentation to isolate critical industrial systems from non-essential networks.

Behavioral Analytics: Deploying behavioral analytics to detect anomalous activities within the industrial network that could indicate a cyber threat.

Incident Response Plan: Establishing a comprehensive incident response plan to ensure swift and effective actions in the event of a security incident.

Lessons Learned:

The industrial IoT security implementation provides crucial lessons, such as:

- Risk Awareness: Conducting thorough risk assessments to identify potential vulnerabilities and prioritize security measures accordingly.

- Cross-Functional Collaboration: Fostering collaboration between IT and OT teams to bridge the gap between information technology and operational technology security.

IV. Smart City Infrastructure: A Robust Urban Ecosystem

Case Study 4: Securing Municipal IoT Deployments

Overview:

A forward-thinking municipality embarked on a journey to transform into a smart city, integrating IoT technologies for enhanced urban services. The security strategy encompassed:

Multi-Layered Authentication: Implementing multi-layered authentication mechanisms to control access to smart city infrastructure, including surveillance cameras and traffic management systems.

Blockchain for Data Integrity: Utilizing blockchain technology to ensure the integrity and transparency of data generated by various municipal IoT devices.

Public Awareness Campaigns: Launching public awareness campaigns to educate citizens about the benefits of smart city technologies and the security measures in place.

Lessons Learned:

The success of securing municipal IoT deployments provides insights, including:

- Community Involvement: Engaging the community in the security process to create a sense of shared responsibility for maintaining a secure urban environment.

- Innovative Technologies: Leveraging cutting-edge technologies like blockchain for data integrity and transparency.

V. Retail IoT: Enhancing Customer Experience Securely

Case Study 5: Retail IoT for Enhanced Customer Engagement

Overview:

A retail chain adopted IoT to enhance customer experience through smart shopping solutions. The security implementation focused on:

Secure Payment Systems: Implementing secure payment gateways and point-of-sale systems to protect customer financial data.

Privacy-Enhancing Technologies: Deploying privacy-enhancing technologies, such as camera anonymization, to balance customer engagement with privacy concerns.

Regular Security Training: Providing regular security training for retail staff to raise awareness about potential threats and best practices.

Lessons Learned:

The retail IoT case study offers valuable lessons, including:

- Privacy-First Approach: Prioritizing customer privacy in IoT implementations, especially in customer-facing applications.

- Employee Awareness: Recognizing the importance of training retail staff to identify and report potential security incidents.

VI. Lessons Learned and Best Practices Across Case Studies

Common Themes and Best Practices:

Risk Assessment as a Foundation: All successful implementations began with a comprehensive risk assessment to identify potential threats and vulnerabilities specific to their environments.

End-to-End Encryption: Protecting data in transit and at rest through robust encryption mechanisms emerged as a consistent best practice.

User Education and Awareness: Implementing ongoing user education and awareness programs played a critical role in ensuring the human element is a security asset rather than a vulnerability.

Adaptive Security Measures: The ability to adapt to evolving threats through continuous monitoring, incident response plans, and dynamic security updates was a common thread.

Cross-Functional Collaboration: Collaboration between different functional areas, including IT and OT, as well as public-private partnerships, was instrumental in successful implementations.

VII. Conclusion: Navigating the Complex Landscape of IoT Security

IoT security implementations are as diverse as the IoT landscape itself. These case studies underscore the importance of a nuanced, adaptive, and holistic approach to security. From critical infrastructure to retail environments, the lessons learned emphasize the need for ongoing vigilance, collaboration, and the integration of security measures throughout the entire IoT ecosystem. As we navigate the complex landscape of IoT security, these case studies provide valuable insights into successful strategies and inspire continued innovation in securing the connected future.

Highlight lessons learned from notable IoT security incidents

The dynamic landscape of the Internet of Things (IoT) brings unprecedented connectivity, efficiency, and innovation. However, it also introduces new dimensions of security challenges. This analysis delves into notable IoT security incidents, unraveling the threads of lessons learned from each scenario. By examining the intricacies of these incidents, we gain insights into the vulnerabilities, consequences, and valuable lessons that shape the ongoing evolution of IoT security.

I. Mirai Botnet: A Wake-Up Call to Insecure IoT Devices

Incident Overview:

The Mirai botnet, in 2016, exploited insecure IoT devices to launch large-scale distributed denial-of-service (DDoS) attacks. Cameras, routers, and other IoT devices with default or weak credentials were compromised, forming a powerful botnet that disrupted major online services.

Lessons Learned:

Credential Management is Crucial: The incident highlighted the critical importance of strong and unique credentials for IoT devices. Manufacturers and users must prioritize robust password policies.

Firmware Updates are Vital: Many compromised devices had outdated firmware. Ensuring prompt and regular firmware updates is essential to patch vulnerabilities and enhance security.

Shared Responsibility: Manufacturers, users, and service providers share responsibility in securing IoT ecosystems. Collaboration is key to addressing vulnerabilities across the supply chain.

II. Stuxnet: Targeting Industrial Control Systems (ICS)

Incident Overview:

Stuxnet, discovered in 2010, was a sophisticated worm designed to target and manipulate industrial control systems, particularly those used in Iran's nuclear program. It highlighted the potential for cyber-physical attacks on critical infrastructure.

Lessons Learned:

Securing Critical Infrastructure is Paramount: Stuxnet emphasized the vulnerability of critical infrastructure to cyberattacks. Robust security measures for industrial control systems are imperative.

Attribution Challenges: The incident underscored the challenges of attributing cyberattacks to specific actors. As IoT deployments grow, addressing attribution becomes increasingly complex.

Need for Defense-in-Depth: Implementing a defense-in-depth strategy, combining network segmentation, intrusion detection, and regular assessments, is crucial for safeguarding critical systems.

III. Dyn Cyberattack: Disrupting Internet Services

Incident Overview:

In 2016, a DDoS attack targeting Dyn, a major DNS service provider, disrupted access to popular websites and online services. The attack leveraged a botnet of compromised IoT devices, illustrating their potential as tools for large-scale disruptions.

Lessons Learned:

IoT Device Security is Collective: The incident showcased the collective impact of insecure IoT devices. Strengthening security requires collaborative efforts from manufacturers, service providers, and users.

Importance of Incident Response: Rapid and effective incident response is essential in mitigating the impact of large-scale IoT-driven attacks. Preparedness and coordination are key components.

Addressing IoT Device End-of-Life: Many compromised devices were outdated and no longer receiving updates. Establishing protocols for end-of-life management is critical to prevent long-term vulnerabilities.

IV. Jeep Cherokee Hack: Demonstrating Vehicle Vulnerabilities

Incident Overview:

In 2015, researchers demonstrated the vulnerability of connected vehicles by remotely hacking a Jeep Cherokee. The incident raised concerns about the security of IoT-enabled vehicles and potential safety risks.

Lessons Learned:

Security-by-Design for IoT Devices: Integrating security measures into the design phase of IoT devices, especially vehicles, is crucial to prevent vulnerabilities.

Collaboration Between Industries: The incident highlighted the need for collaboration between the automotive and cybersecurity industries to establish robust standards and practices.

Ongoing Monitoring and Updates: Continuous monitoring of connected vehicles and the ability to push security updates remotely are essential components of automotive cybersecurity.

V. Nest Camera Incidents: Invasion of Privacy

Incident Overview:

Several incidents involving compromised Nest cameras raised concerns about unauthorized access and invasion of user privacy. Incidents included instances of strangers speaking to individuals through compromised cameras.

Lessons Learned:

Secure Default Settings: Manufacturers must ensure that default settings for IoT devices prioritize security, including strong authentication measures.

User Awareness and Education: Educating users about the importance of changing default passwords, enabling two-factor authentication, and understanding privacy settings is crucial.

Transparent Communication: When incidents occur, transparent communication from manufacturers about the nature of the breach and steps taken to address it builds trust with users.

VI. Lessons Synthesized and Emerging Best Practices
Common Threads Across Incidents:

Security is a Shared Responsibility: Whether in manufacturing, usage, or service provision, all stakeholders play a role in ensuring IoT security.

Firmware and Software Updates are Critical: Regular updates are essential to address vulnerabilities and enhance the resilience of IoT ecosystems.

User Education is Paramount: User awareness about security practices, from password management to privacy settings, is a foundational element of IoT security.

Emerging Best Practices:

Security-by-Design Principles: Embedding security measures into the design and development phases of IoT devices ensures a proactive rather than reactive security posture.

Industry Collaboration: Cross-industry collaboration is essential to establish standardized security practices and address the evolving threat landscape.

Ethical Hacking and Red Teaming: Proactive testing through ethical hacking and red teaming helps identify vulnerabilities before they can be exploited maliciously.

VII. Conclusion: A Continual Journey of Improvement
IoT security incidents provide a valuable source of learning, driving continuous improvement in the field. As technology evolves, so do the threats, emphasizing the need for an

adaptive and collaborative approach. By dissecting these incidents and distilling lessons, the IoT community can collectively work towards fortifying the connected future.

Key takeaways for readers to apply in their own IoT security strategies

The intricate tapestry of IoT security incidents provides more than cautionary tales; it offers a wealth of practical insights. By distilling key takeaways from these real-world scenarios, we can pave the way for readers to fortify their own IoT security strategies. This analysis synthesizes actionable lessons, providing a roadmap for addressing vulnerabilities, enhancing resilience, and fostering a proactive security posture in the ever-evolving landscape of the Internet of Things.

I. User Authentication and Credential Management

   Lessons from Mirai Botnet:

*   Key Takeaway: Prioritize robust user authentication and credential management for all IoT devices.
*   Implementation Strategies:
*   Enforce strong, unique passwords for IoT devices.
*   Encourage users to change default credentials during setup.
*   Implement multi-factor authentication where feasible.

   Lessons from Nest Camera Incidents:

*   Key Takeaway: Default settings matter; secure them intelligently to prevent unauthorized access.
*   Implementation Strategies:
*   Design devices with secure default settings.

- Educate users on the importance of changing default passwords.

II. Firmware and Software Updates

Lessons from Mirai Botnet and Dyn Cyberattack:

- Key Takeaway: Regularly update firmware and software to patch vulnerabilities.
- Implementation Strategies:
- Establish automated update mechanisms for IoT devices.
- Clearly communicate the importance of updates to users.

Lessons from Stuxnet:

- Key Takeaway: Firmware updates should be part of a holistic defense strategy for critical infrastructure.
- Implementation Strategies:
- Conduct thorough risk assessments for critical systems.
- Integrate firmware updates into overall security protocols.

III. End-of-Life Management

Lessons from Dyn Cyberattack:

- Key Takeaway: Develop protocols for secure decommissioning of IoT devices at the end of their lifecycle.
- Implementation Strategies:
- Provide clear guidelines for users on retiring IoT devices.
- Ensure end-of-life procedures include security measures.

Lessons from Jeep Cherokee Hack:

- Key Takeaway: Address vulnerabilities in outdated devices to prevent long-term risks.
- Implementation Strategies:

175

● Monitor the lifecycle of IoT devices and plan for their secure retirement.

● Collaborate with manufacturers to ensure ongoing support.

IV. Security-by-Design Principles

Lessons from Stuxnet and Jeep Cherokee Hack:

● Key Takeaway: Embed security measures into the design phase of IoT devices.

● Implementation Strategies:

● Prioritize security features during the development process.

● Involve cybersecurity experts in the design phase.

Lessons from Nest Camera Incidents:

● Key Takeaway: Transparent communication is crucial when security incidents occur.

● Implementation Strategies:

● Establish clear communication channels with users in the event of a security breach.

● Provide timely and transparent information on remedial actions taken.

V. Cross-Industry Collaboration

Lessons from Stuxnet and Dyn Cyberattack:

● Key Takeaway: Collaboration between industries is essential to establish standardized security practices.

● Implementation Strategies:

● Foster partnerships between IoT manufacturers, service providers, and cybersecurity experts.

● Advocate for cross-industry initiatives to address shared challenges.

Lessons from Jeep Cherokee Hack:

● Key Takeaway: Collaboration between the automotive and cybersecurity industries is crucial.

176

- Implementation Strategies:
- Establish forums for continuous dialogue between automotive and cybersecurity professionals.
- Develop industry-wide standards for automotive cybersecurity.

VI. Ethical Hacking and Red Teaming

Lessons from Mirai Botnet and Stuxnet:

- Key Takeaway: Proactive testing through ethical hacking and red teaming helps identify vulnerabilities.
- Implementation Strategies:
- Integrate ethical hacking as a regular practice in security protocols.
- Engage external security experts for red teaming exercises.

Lessons from Dyn Cyberattack:

- Key Takeaway: Rapid and effective incident response is essential in mitigating large-scale attacks.
- Implementation Strategies:
- Develop and regularly update incident response plans.
- Conduct simulated exercises to test the efficacy of response strategies.

VII. User Education and Awareness

Lessons from Nest Camera Incidents:

- Key Takeaway: User education is foundational for IoT security.
- Implementation Strategies:
- Develop user-friendly educational materials on IoT security best practices.
- Conduct regular awareness campaigns for device users.

Lessons Synthesized and Emerging Best Practices:

- Key Takeaway: Security is a shared responsibility, requiring collaboration between manufacturers, service providers, and users.
- Implementation Strategies:
- Establish community forums for sharing best practices.
- Include security awareness as part of product documentation and user interfaces.

VIII. Conclusion: Navigating the Path to Secure IoT Deployments

As we navigate the path to secure IoT deployments, these actionable takeaways serve as guideposts. Implementing robust user authentication, embracing security-by-design principles, and fostering cross-industry collaboration are not isolated tasks; they are interconnected components of a resilient IoT security strategy. By incorporating these insights into their approach, readers can fortify their IoT ecosystems against evolving threats, ensuring a connected future that is secure, trustworthy, and resilient.

Bibliography

"Automotive Cybersecurity: From Perimeter Defense to Resilience", Author: Josh Corman, Philip Agcaoili, Jeff Williams, et al., Publisher: O'Reilly Media, Year: 2020

"The Car Hacker's Handbook: A Guide for the Penetration Tester", Author: Craig Smith, Publisher: No Starch Press, Year: 2016

"Automotive Cybersecurity and Connected Car Hacking", Author: Dr. Steffen Wendzel, Publisher: Apress, Year: 2016

"Introduction to Autonomous Vehicles", Author: Saswat Chakrabarti, Publisher: CRC Press, Year: 2020

"IoT Security: A Guide for IT and Security Professionals", Author: James A. Martin, Publisher: Wiley, Year: 2018

"Security Engineering: A Guide to Building Dependable Distributed Systems", Author: Ross J. Anderson, Publisher: Wiley, Year: 2020

"Building the Internet of Things: Implement New Business Models, Disrupt Competitors, Transform Your Industry", Author: Maciej Kranz, Publisher: Wiley, Year: 2016

"IoT Inc: How Your Company Can Use the Internet of Things to Win in the Outcome Economy", Author: Bruce Sinclair, Publisher: McGraw-Hill Education, Year: 2017

"Future Crimes: Everything Is Connected, Everyone Is Vulnerable and What We Can Do About It", Author: Marc Goodman, Publisher: Anchor, Year: 2016

"Hacking: The Art of Exploitation", Author: Jon Erickson, Publisher: No Starch Press, Year: 2008